T0144819

# The Melting Pot

# The Melting Pot
Israel Zangwill

MINT EDITIONS

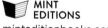

*The Melting Pot* was first published in 1909.

This edition published by Mint Editions 2021.

ISBN 9781513134024

Published by Mint Editions®

**MINT EDITIONS**

minteditionbooks.com

Publishing Director: Jennifer Newens
Design & Production: Rachel Lopez Metzger
Project Manager: Micaela Clark
Typesetting: Westchester Publishing Services

# THE CAST

| | |
|---|---|
| David Quixano | WALKER WHITESIDE |
| Mendel Quixano | HENRY BERGMAN |
| Baron Revendal | JOHN BLAIR |
| Quincy Davenport, Jr. | GRANT STEWART |
| Herr Pappelmeister | HENRY VOGEL |
| Vera Revendal | CHRYSTAL HERNE |
| Baroness Revendal | LEONORA VON OTTINGER |
| Frau Quixano | LOUISE MULDENER |
| Kathleen O'Reilly | MOLLIE REVEL |
| Settlement Servant | ANNIE HARRIS |
| David Quixano | HAROLD CHAPIN |
| Mendel Quixano | HUGH TABBERER |
| Baron Revendal | H. LAWRENCE LEYTON |
| Quincy Davenport, Jr. | P. PERCEVAL CLARK |
| Herr Pappelmeister | CLIFTON ALDERSON |
| Vera Revendal | PHYLLIS RELPH |
| Baroness Revendal | GILLIAN SCAIFE |
| Frau Quixano | INEZ BENSUSAN |
| Kathleen O'Reilly | E. NOLAN O'CONNOR |
| Settlement Servant | RUTH PARROTT |

# Act I

*The scene is laid in the living-room of the small home of the* QUIXANOS *in the Richmond or non-Jewish borough of New York, about five o'clock of a February afternoon. At centre back is a double street-door giving on a columned veranda in the Colonial style. Nailed on the right-hand door-post gleams a* Mezuzah, *a tiny metal case, containing a Biblical passage. On the right of the door is a small hat-stand holding* MENDEL'S *overcoat, umbrella, etc. There are two windows, one on either side of the door, and three exits, one down-stage on the left leading to the stairs and family bedrooms, and two on the right, the upper leading to* KATHLEEN'S *bedroom and the lower to the kitchen. Over the street door is pinned the Stars-and-Stripes. On the left wall, in the upper corner of which is a music-stand, are bookshelves of large mouldering Hebrew books, and over them is hung a* Mizrach, *or Hebrew picture, to show it is the East Wall. Other pictures round the room include Wagner, Columbus, Lincoln, and "Jews at the Wailing place." Downstage, about a yard from the left wall, stands* DAVID'S *roll-desk, open and displaying a medley of music, a quill pen, etc. On the wall behind the desk hangs a book-rack with brightly bound English books. A grand piano stands at left centre back, holding a pile of music and one huge Hebrew tome. There is a table in the middle of the room covered with a red cloth and a litter of objects, music, and newspapers. The fireplace, in which a fire is burning, occupies the centre of the right wall, and by it stands an armchair on which lies another heavy mouldy Hebrew tome. The mantel holds a clock, two silver candlesticks, etc. A chiffonier stands against the back wall on the right. There are a few cheap chairs. The whole effect is a curious blend of shabbiness, Americanism, Jewishness, and music, all four being combined in the figure of* MENDEL QUIXANO, *who, in a black skull-cap, a seedy velvet jacket, and red carpet-slippers, is discovered standing at the open street-door. He is an elderly music master with a fine Jewish face, pathetically furrowed by misfortunes, and a short grizzled beard.*

MENDEL: Good-bye, Johnny! . . . And don't forget to practise your scales.
(*Shutting door, shivers*)
  Ugh! It'll snow again, I guess.
(*He yawns, heaves a great sigh of relief, walks toward the table, and perceives a music-roll*)
  The chump! He's forgotten his music!

(*He picks it up and runs toward the window on the left, muttering furiously*)

Brainless, earless, thumb-fingered Gentile!

(*Throwing open the window*)

Here, Johnny! You can't practise your scales if you leave 'em here!

(*He throws out the music-roll and shivers again at the cold as he shuts the window*)

Ugh! And I must go out to that miserable dancing class to scrape the rent together.

(*He goes to the fire and warms his hands*)

*Ach Gott!* What a life! What a life!

(*He drops dejectedly into the armchair. Finding himself sitting uncomfortably on the big book, he half rises and pushes it to the side of the seat. After an instant an irate Irish voice is heard from behind the kitchen door*)

KATHLEEN (*Without*): Divil take the butther! I wouldn't put up with ye, not for a hundred dollars a week.

MENDEL (*Raising himself to listen, heaves great sigh*): *Ach!* Mother and Kathleen again!

KATHLEEN (*Still louder*): Pots and pans and plates and knives! Sure 'tis enough to make a saint chrazy.

FRAU QUIXANO (*Equally loudly from kitchen*): *Wos schreist du? Gott in Himmel, dieses Amerika!*

KATHLEEN (*Opening door of kitchen toward the end of* FRAU QUIXANO'S *speech, but turning back, with her hand visible on the door*): What's that ye're afther jabberin' about America? If ye don't like God's own counthry, sure ye can go back to your own Jerusalem, so ye can.

MENDEL: One's very servants are anti-Semites.

KATHLEEN (*Bangs her door as she enters excitedly, carrying a folded white table-cloth. She is a young and pretty Irish maid-of-all-work*): Bad luck to me, if iver I take sarvice again with haythen Jews.

(*She perceives* MENDEL *huddled up in the armchair, gives a little scream, and drops the cloth*)

Och, I thought ye was out!

MENDEL (*Rising*): And so you dared to be rude to my mother.

KATHLEEN (*Angrily, as she picks up the cloth*): She said I put mate on a butther-plate.

MENDEL: Well, you know that's against her religion.

KATHLEEN: But I didn't do nothing of the soort. I ounly put butther on a mate-plate.

MENDEL: That's just as bad. What the Bible forbids—

KATHLEEN (*Lays the cloth on a chair and vigorously clears off the litter of things on the table*): Sure, the Pope himself couldn't remimber it all. Why don't ye have a sinsible religion?

MENDEL: You are impertinent. Attend to your work.

(*He seats himself at the piano*)

KATHLEEN: And isn't it laying the Sabbath cloth I am?

(*She bangs down articles from the table into their right places*)

MENDEL: Don't answer me back.

(*He begins to play softly*)

KATHLEEN: Faith, I must answer *somebody* back—and sorra a word of English *she* understands. I might as well talk to a tree.

MENDEL: You are not paid to talk, but to work.

(*Playing on softly*)

KATHLEEN: And who *can* work wid an ould woman nagglin' and grizzlin' and faultin' me?

(*She removes the red table-cloth*)

Mate-plates, butther-plates, *kosher*, *trepha*, sure I've smashed up folks' crockery and they makin' less fuss ouver it.

MENDEL (*Stops playing*): Breaking crockery is one thing, and breaking a religion another. Didn't you tell me when I engaged you that you had lived in other Jewish families?

KATHLEEN (*Angrily*): And is it a liar ye'd make me out now? I've lived wid clothiers and pawnbrokers and Vaudeville actors, but I niver shtruck a house where mate and butther couldn't be as paceable on the same plate as eggs and bacon—the most was that some wouldn't ate the bacon onless 'twas killed *kosher*.

MENDEL (*Tickled*): Ha! Ha! Ha! Ha! Ha!

KATHLEEN (*Furious, pauses with the white table-cloth half on*): And who's ye laughin' at? I give ye a week's notice. I won't be the joke of Jews, no, begorra, that I won't.

(*She pulls the cloth on viciously*)

MENDEL (*Sobered, rising from the piano*): Don't talk nonsense, Kathleen. Nobody is making a joke of you. Have a little patience—you'll soon learn our ways.

KATHLEEN (*More mildly*): Whose ways, yours or the ould lady's or Mr. David's? To-night being yer Sabbath, *you'll* be blowing out yer bedroom candle, though ye won't light it; Mr. David'll light his and blow it out too; and the misthress won't even touch the candleshtick. There's three religions in this house, not wan.

MENDEL (*Coughs uneasily*): Hem! Well, you learn the mistress's ways—that will be enough.

KATHLEEN (*Going to mantelpiece*): But what way can I understand her jabberin' and jibberin'?—I'm not a monkey!

(*She takes up a silver candlestick*)

Why doesn't she talk English like a Christian?

MENDEL (*Irritated*): If you are going on like that, perhaps you had better *not* remain here.

KATHLEEN (*Blazing up, forgetting to take the second candlestick*): And who's axin' ye to remain here? Faith, I'll quit off this blissid minit!

MENDEL (*Taken aback*): No, you can't do that.

KATHLEEN: And why can't I? Ye can keep yer dirthy wages.

(*She dumps down the candlestick violently on the table, and exit hysterically into her bedroom*)

MENDEL (*Sighing heavily*): She might have put on the other candlestick.

(*He goes to mantel and takes it. A rat-tat-tat at street-door*)

Who can that be?

(*Running to* KATHLEEN'S *door, holding candlestick forgetfully low*)

Kathleen! There's a visitor!

KATHLEEN (*Angrily from within*): I'm not here!

MENDEL: So long as you're in this house, you must do your work.

(KATHLEEN'S *head emerges sulkily*)

KATHLEEN: I tould ye I was lavin' at wanst. Let you open the door yerself.

MENDEL: I'm not dressed to receive visitors—it may be a new pupil.

(*He goes toward staircase, automatically carrying off the candlestick which* KATHLEEN *has not caught sight of. Exit on the left*)

KATHLEEN (*Moving toward the street-door*): The divil fly away wid me if ivir from this 'our I set foot again among haythen furriners—

(*She throws open the door angrily and then the outer door.* VERA REVENDAL, *a beautiful girl in furs and muff, with a touch of the exotic in her appearance, steps into the little vestibule*)

VERA: Is Mr. Quixano at home?

KATHLEEN (*Sulkily*): Which Mr. Quixano?

VERA (*Surprised*): Are there two Mr. Quixanos?

KATHLEEN (*Tartly*): Didn't I say there was?

VERA: Then I want the one who plays.

KATHLEEN: There isn't a one who plays.

VERA: Oh, surely!

KATHLEEN: Ye're wrong entirely. They both plays.

VERA (*Smiling*): Oh, dear! And I suppose they both play the violin.

KATHLEEN: Ye're wrong again. One plays the piano—ounly the young ginthleman plays the fiddle—Mr. David!

VERA (*Eagerly*): Ah, Mr. David—that's the one I want to see.

KATHLEEN: He's out.

(*She abruptly shuts the door*)

VERA (*Stopping its closing*): Don't shut the door!

KATHLEEN (*Snappily*): More chanst of seeing him out there than in here!

VERA: But I want to leave a message.

KATHLEEN: Then why don't ye come inside? It's freezin' me to the bone.

(*She sneezes*)

Atchoo!

VERA: I'm sorry.

(*She comes in and closes the door*)

Will you please say Miss Revendal called from the Settlement, and we are anxiously awaiting his answer to the letter asking him to play for us on—

KATHLEEN: What way will I be tellin' him all that? I'm not here.

VERA: Eh?

KATHLEEN: I'm lavin'—just as soon as I've me thrunk packed.

VERA: Then I must *write* the message—can I write at this desk?

KATHLEEN: If the ould woman don't come in and shpy you.

VERA: What old woman?

KATHLEEN: Ould Mr. Quixano's mother—she wears a black wig, she's that houly.

VERA (*Bewildered*): What? . . . But why should she mind my writing?

KATHLEEN: Look at the clock.

(VERA *looks at the clock, more puzzled than ever*)

If ye're not quick, it'll be *Shabbos*.

VERA: Be what?

KATHLEEN (*Holds up hands of horror*): Ye don't know what *Shabbos* is! A Jewess not know her own Sunday!

VERA (*Outraged*): I, a Jewess! How dare you?

KATHLEEN (*Flustered*): Axin' your pardon, miss, but ye looked a bit furrin and I—

VERA (*Frozen*): I am a Russian.

(*Slowly and dazedly*)

Do I understand that Mr. Quixano is a Jew?

KATHLEEN: Two Jews, miss. Both of 'em.

VERA: Oh, but it is impossible.

(*Dazedly to herself*)

He had such charming manners.

(*Aloud again*)

You seem to think everybody Jewish. Are you sure Mr. Quixano is not Spanish?—the name sounds Spanish.

KATHLEEN: Shpanish!

(*She picks up the old Hebrew book on the armchair*)

Look at the ould lady's book. Is that Shpanish?

(*She points to the Mizrach*)

And that houly picture the ould lady says her pater-noster to! Is that Shpanish? And that houly table-cloth with the houly silver candle—

(*Cry of sudden astonishment*)

Why, I've ounly put—

(*She looks toward mantel and utters a great cry of alarm as she drops the Hebrew book on the floor*)

Why, where's the other candleshtick! Mother in hivin, they'll say I shtole the candleshtick!

(*Perceiving that* VERA *is dazedly moving toward door*)

Beggin' your pardon, miss—

(*She is about to move a chair toward the desk*)

VERA: Thank you, I've changed my mind.

KATHLEEN: That's more than I'll do.

VERA (*Hand on door*): Don't say I called at all.

KATHLEEN: Plaze yerself. What name did ye say?

(MENDEL *enters hastily from his bedroom, completely transmogrified, minus the skull-cap, with a Prince Albert coat, and boots instead of slippers, so that his appearance is gentlemanly.* KATHLEEN *begins to search quietly and unostentatiously in the table-drawers, the chiffonier, etc., etc., for the candlestick*)

MENDEL: I am sorry if I have kept you waiting—

(*He rubs his hands importantly*)

You see I have so many pupils already. Won't you sit down?

(*He indicates a chair*)

VERA (*Flushing, embarrassed, releasing her hold of the door handle*): Thank you—I—I—I didn't come about pianoforte lessons.

MENDEL (*Sighing in disappointment*): *Ach!*

VERA: In fact I—er—it wasn't you I wanted at all—I was just going.

MENDEL (*Politely*): Perhaps I can direct you to the house you are looking for.

VERA: Thank you, I won't trouble you.

(*She turns toward the door again*)

MENDEL: Allow me!

(*He opens the door for her*)

VERA (*Hesitating, struck by his manners, struggling with her anti-Jewish prejudice*): It—it—was your son I wanted.

MENDEL (*His face lighting up*): You mean my nephew, David. Yes, *he* gives violin lessons.

(*He closes the door*)

VERA: Oh, is he your nephew?

MENDEL: I am sorry he is out—he, too, has so many pupils, though at the moment he is only at the Crippled Children's Home—playing to them.

VERA: How lovely of him!

(*Touched and deciding to conquer her prejudice*)

But that's just what *I* came about—I mean we'd like him to play again at our Settlement. Please ask him why he hasn't answered Miss Andrews's letter.

MENDEL (*Astonished*): He hasn't answered your letter?

VERA: Oh, I'm not Miss Andrews; I'm only her assistant.

MENDEL: I see—Kathleen, whatever are you doing under the table?

(KATHLEEN, *in her hunting around for the candlestick, is now stooping and lifting up the table-cloth*)

KATHLEEN: Sure the fiend's after witching away the candleshtick.

MENDEL (*Embarrassed*): The candlestick? Oh—I—I think you'll find it in my bedroom.

KATHLEEN: Wisha, now!

(*She goes into his bedroom*)

MENDEL (*Turning apologetically to* VERA): I beg your pardon, Miss Andrews, I mean Miss—er—

VERA: Revendal.

MENDEL (*Slightly more interested*): Revendal? Then you must be the Miss Revendal David told me about!

VERA (*Blushing*): Why, he has only seen me once—the time he played at our Roof-Garden Concert.

MENDEL: Yes, but he was so impressed by the way you handled those new immigrants—the Spirit of the Settlement, he called you.

VERA (*Modestly*): Ah, no—Miss Andrews is that. And you will tell him to answer her letter at once, won't you, because there's only a week now to our Concert.

(*A gust of wind shakes the windows. She smiles*)

Naturally it will *not* be on the Roof Garden.

MENDEL (*Half to himself*): Fancy David not saying a word about it to me! Are you sure the letter was mailed?

VERA: I mailed it myself—a week ago. And even in New York—

(*She smiles. Re-enter* KATHLEEN *with the recovered candlestick*)

KATHLEEN: Bedad, ye're as great a shleep-walker as Mr. David!

(*She places the candlestick on the table and moves toward her bedroom*)

MENDEL: Kathleen!

KATHLEEN (*Pursuing her walk without turning*): I'm not here!

MENDEL: Did you take in a letter for Mr. David about a week ago?

(*Smiling at* MISS REVENDAL)

He doesn't get many, you see.

KATHLEEN (*Turning*): A letter? Sure, I took in ounly a postcard from Miss Johnson, an' that ounly sayin'—

VERA: And you don't remember a letter—a large letter—last Saturday—with the seal of our Settlement?

KATHLEEN: Last Saturday wid a seal, is it? Sure, how could I forgit it?

MENDEL: Then you *did* take it in?

KATHLEEN: Ye're wrong entirely. 'Twas the misthress took it in.

MENDEL (*To* VERA): I am sorry the boy has been so rude.

KATHLEEN: But the misthress didn't give it him at wanst—she hid it away bekaz it was *Shabbos*.

MENDEL: Oh, dear—and she has forgotten to give it to him. Excuse me.

(*He makes a hurried exit to the kitchen*)

KATHLEEN: And excuse *me*—I've me thrunk to pack.

(*She goes toward her bedroom, pauses at the door*)

And ye'll witness I don't pack the candleshtick.

(*Emphatic exit*)

VERA (*Still dazed*): A Jew! That wonderful boy a Jew! . . . But then so was David the shepherd youth with his harp and his psalms, the sweet singer in Israel.

(*She surveys the room and its contents with interest. The windows rattle once or twice in the rising wind. The light gets gradually less. She picks up the huge Hebrew tome on the piano and puts it down with a slight smile as if overwhelmed by the weight of alien antiquity. Then she goes over to the desk and picks up the printed music*)

Mendelssohn's Concerto, Tartini's Sonata in G Minor, Bach's Chaconne. . .

(*She looks up at the book-rack*)

"History of the American Commonwealth," "Cyclopædia of History,"

"History of the Jews"—he seems very fond of history. Ah, there's Shelley and Tennyson.

(*With surprise*)

Nietzsche next to the Bible? No Russian books apparently—

(*Re-enter* MENDEL *triumphantly with a large sealed letter*)

MENDEL: Here it is! As it came on Saturday, my mother was afraid David would open it!

VERA (*Smiling*): But what *can* you do with a letter except open it? Any more than with an oyster?

MENDEL (*Smiling as he puts the letter on* DAVID'*s desk*): To a pious Jew letters and oysters are alike forbidden—at least letters may not be opened on our day of rest.

VERA: I'm sure I couldn't rest till I'd opened mine.

(*Enter from the kitchen* FRAU QUIXANO, *defending herself with excited gesticulation. She is an old lady with a black wig, but her appearance is dignified, venerable even, in no way comic. She speaks Yiddish exclusively, that being largely the language of the Russian Pale*)

FRAU QUIXANO: *Obber ich hob gesogt zu Kathleen—*

MENDEL (*Turning and going to her*): Yes, yes, mother, that's all right now.

FRAU QUIXANO (*In horror, perceiving her Hebrew book on the floor, where* KATHLEEN *has dropped it*): *Mein Buch!*

(*She picks it up and kisses it piously*)

MENDEL (*Presses her into her fireside chair*): *Ruhig, ruhig, Mutter!*

(*To* VERA)

She understands barely a word of English—she won't disturb us.

VERA: Oh, but I must be going—I was so long finding the house, and look! it has begun to snow!

(*They both turn their heads and look at the falling snow*)

MENDEL: All the more reason to wait for David—it may leave off. He can't be long now. Do sit down.

(*He offers a chair*)

FRAU QUIXANO (*Looking round suspiciously*): *Wos will die Shikseh?*

VERA: What does your mother say?

MENDEL (*Half-smiling*): Oh, only asking what your heathen ladyship desires.

VERA: Tell her I hope she is well.

MENDEL: *Das Fräulein hofft dass es geht gut—*

FRAU QUIXANO (*Shrugging her shoulders in despairing astonishment*): *Gut? Un' wie soll es gut gehen—in Amerika!*

(*She takes out her spectacles, and begins slowly polishing and adjusting them*)

VERA (*Smiling*): I understood that last word.

MENDEL: She asks how can anything possibly go well in America!

VERA: Ah, she doesn't like America.

MENDEL (*Half-smiling*): Her favourite exclamation is "*A Klog zu Columbessen!*"

VERA: What does that mean?

MENDEL: Cursed be Columbus!

VERA (*Laughingly*): Poor Columbus! I suppose she's just come over.

MENDEL: Oh, no, it must be ten years since I sent for her.

VERA: Really! But your nephew was born here?

MENDEL: No, he's Russian too. But please sit down, you had better get his answer at once.

(VERA *sits*)

VERA: I suppose *you* taught him music.

MENDEL: I? I can't play the violin. He is self-taught. In the Russian Pale he was a wonder-child. Poor David! He always looked forward to coming to America; he imagined I was a famous musician over here. He found me conductor in a cheap theatre—a converted beer-hall.

VERA: Was he very disappointed?

MENDEL: Disappointed? He was enchanted! He is crazy about America.

VERA (*Smiling*): Ah, *he* doesn't curse Columbus.

MENDEL: My mother came with her life behind her: David with his life before him. Poor boy!

VERA: Why do you say poor boy?

MENDEL: What is there before him here but a terrible struggle for life? If he doesn't curse Columbus, he'll curse fate. Music-lessons and dance-halls, beer-halls and weddings—every hope and ambition will be ground out of him, and he will die obscure and unknown.

(*His head sinks on his breast,* FRAU QUIXANO *is heard faintly sobbing over her book. The sobbing continues throughout the scene*)

VERA (*Half rising*): You have made your mother cry.

MENDEL: Oh, no—she understood nothing. She always cries on the eve of the Sabbath.

VERA (*Mystified, sinking back into her chair*): Always cries? Why?

MENDEL (*Embarrassed*): Oh, well, a Christian wouldn't understand—

VERA: Yes I could—do tell me!

MENDEL: She knows that in this great grinding America, David and I must go out to earn our bread on Sabbath as on week-days. She never says a word to us, but her heart is full of tears.

VERA: Poor old woman. It was wrong of us to ask your nephew to play at the Settlement for nothing.

MENDEL (*Rising fiercely*): If you offer him a fee, he shall not play. Did you think I was begging of you?

VERA: I beg your pardon—

(*She smiles*)

There, *I* am begging of *you*. Sit down, please.

MENDEL (*Walking away to piano*): I ought not to have burdened you with our troubles—you are too young.

VERA (*Pathetically*): I young? If you only knew how old I am!

MENDEL: You?

VERA: I left my youth in Russia—eternities ago.

MENDEL: You know our Russia!

(*He goes over to her and sits down*)

VERA: Can't you see I'm a Russian, too?

(*With a faint tremulous smile*)

I might even have been a Siberian had I stayed. But I escaped from my gaolers.

MENDEL: You were a Revolutionist!

VERA: Who can live in Russia and not be? So you see trouble and I are not such strangers.

MENDEL: Who would have thought it to look at you? Siberia, gaolers, revolutions!

(*Rising*)

What terrible things life holds!

VERA: Yes, even in free America.

(FRAU QUIXANO's *sobbing grows slightly louder*)

MENDEL: That Settlement work must be full of tragedies.

VERA: Sometimes one sees nothing but the tragedy of things.

(*Looking toward the window*)

  The snow is getting thicker. How pitilessly it falls—like fate.

MENDEL (*Following her gaze*): Yes, icy and inexorable.

(*The faint sobbing of* FRAU QUIXANO *over her book, which has been heard throughout the scene as a sort of musical accompaniment, has combined to work it up to a mood of intense sadness, intensified by the growing dusk, so that as the two now gaze at the falling snow, the atmosphere seems overbrooded with melancholy. There is a moment or two without dialogue, given over to the sobbing of* FRAU QUIXANO, *the roar of the wind shaking the windows, the quick falling of the snow. Suddenly a happy voice singing "My Country 'tis of Thee" is heard from without*)

FRAU QUIXANO (*Pricking up her ears, joyously*): *Do ist Dovidel!*

MENDEL: That's David!

(*He springs up*)

VERA (*Murmurs in relief*): Ah!

(*The whole atmosphere is changed to one of joyous expectation,* DAVID *is seen and heard passing the left window, still singing the national hymn, but it breaks off abruptly as he throws open the door and appears on the threshold, a buoyant snow-covered figure in a cloak and a broad-brimmed hat, carrying a violin case. He is a sunny, handsome youth of the finest Russo-Jewish type. He speaks with a slight German accent*)

DAVID: Isn't it a beautiful world, uncle?

(*He closes the inner door*)

  Snow, the divine white snow—

(*Perceiving the visitor with amaze*)

  Miss Revendal here!

(*He removes his hat and looks at her with boyish reverence and wonder*)

VERA (*Smiling*): Don't look so surprised—I haven't fallen from heaven like the snow.

  Take off your wet things.

DAVID: Oh, it's nothing; it's dry snow.

(*He lays down his violin case and brushes off the snow from his cloak, which* MENDEL *takes from him and hangs on the rack, all without interrupting the dialogue*)

  If I had only known you were waiting—

VERA: I am glad you didn't—I wouldn't have had those poor little cripples cheated out of a moment of your music.

DAVID: Uncle has told you? Ah, it was bully! You should have seen the cripples waltzing with their crutches!

(*He has moved toward the old woman, and while he holds one hand to the blaze now pats her cheek with the other in greeting, to which she responds with a loving smile ere she settles contentedly to slumber over her book*)

*Es war grossartig*, Granny. Even the paralysed danced.

MENDEL: Don't exaggerate, David.

DAVID: Exaggerate, uncle! Why, if they hadn't the use of their legs, their arms danced on the counterpane; if their arms couldn't dance, their hands danced from the wrist; and if their hands couldn't dance, they danced with their fingers; and if their fingers couldn't dance, their heads danced; and if their heads were paralysed, why, their eyes danced—God never curses so utterly but you've *something* left to dance with!

(*He moves toward his desk*)

VERA (*Infected with his gaiety*): You'll tell us next the beds danced.

DAVID: So they did—they shook their legs like mad!

VERA: Oh, why wasn't I there?

(*His eyes meet hers at the thought of her presence*)

DAVID: Dear little cripples, I felt as if I could play them all straight again with the love and joy jumping out of this old fiddle.

(*He lays his hand caressingly on the violin*)

MENDEL (*Gloomily*): But in reality you left them as crooked as ever.

DAVID: No, I didn't.

(*He caresses the back of his uncle's head in affectionate rebuke*)

I couldn't play their bones straight, but I played their brains straight. And hunch-*brains* are worse than hunch-*backs*. . .

(*Suddenly perceiving his letter on the desk*)

A letter for *me*!

(*He takes it with boyish eagerness, then hesitates to open it*)

VERA (*Smiling*): Oh, you may open it!

DAVID (*Wistfully*): May I?

VERA (*Smiling*): Yes, and quick—or it'll be *Shabbos*!

(DAVID *looks up at her in wonder*)

MENDEL (*Smiling*): You read your letter!

DAVID (*Opens it eagerly, then smiles broadly with pleasure*): Oh, Miss Revendal! Isn't that great! To play again at your Settlement. I *am* getting famous.

VERA: But we can't offer you a fee.

MENDEL (*Quickly sotto voce to* VERA): Thank you!

DAVID: A fee! I'd pay a fee to see all those happy immigrants you gather together—Dutchmen and Greeks, Poles and Norwegians, Welsh and Armenians. If you only had Jews, it would be as good as going to Ellis Island.

VERA (*Smiling*): What a strange taste! Who on earth wants to go to Ellis Island?

DAVID: Oh, I love going to Ellis Island to watch the ships coming in from Europe, and to think that all those weary, sea-tossed wanderers are feeling what *I* felt when America first stretched out her great mother-hand to *me*!

VERA (*Softly*): Were you very happy?

DAVID: It was heaven. You must remember that all my life I had heard of America—everybody in our town had friends there or was going there or got money orders from there. The earliest game I played at was selling off my toy furniture and setting up in America. All my life America was waiting, beckoning, shining—the place where God would wipe away tears from off all faces.

(*He ends in a half-sob*)

MENDEL (*Rises, as in terror*): Now, now, David, don't get excited.

(*Approaches him*)

DAVID: To think that the same great torch of liberty which threw its light across all the broad seas and lands into my little garret in Russia, is shining also for all those other weeping millions of Europe, shining wherever men hunger and are oppressed—

MENDEL (*Soothingly*): Yes, yes, David.

(*Laying hand on his shoulder*)

Now sit down and—

DAVID (*Unheeding*): Shining over the starving villages of Italy and Ireland, over the swarming stony cities of Poland and Galicia, over the ruined farms of Roumania, over the shambles of Russia—

MENDEL (*Pleadingly*): David!

DAVID: Oh, Miss Revendal, when I look at our Statue of Liberty, I just seem to hear the voice of America crying: "Come unto me all ye that labour and are heavy laden and I will give you rest—rest—"

ISRAEL ZANGWILL

(*He is now almost sobbing*)

MENDEL: Don't talk any more—you know it is bad for you.

DAVID: But Miss Revendal asked—and I want to explain to her what America means to me.

MENDEL: You can explain it in your American symphony.

VERA (*Eagerly—to* DAVID): You compose?

DAVID (*Embarrassed*): Oh, uncle, why did you talk of—? Uncle always—my music is so thin and tinkling. When I am *writing* my American symphony, it seems like thunder crashing through a forest full of bird songs. But next day—oh, next day!

(*He laughs dolefully and turns away*)

VERA: So your music finds inspiration in America?

DAVID: Yes—in the seething of the Crucible.

VERA: The Crucible? I don't understand!

DAVID: Not understand! You, the Spirit of the Settlement!

(*He rises and crosses to her and leans over the table, facing her*)

Not understand that America is God's Crucible, the great Melting-Pot where all the races of Europe are melting and re-forming! Here you stand, good folk, think I, when I see them at Ellis Island, here you stand

(*Graphically illustrating it on the table*)

in your fifty groups, with your fifty languages and histories, and your fifty blood hatreds and rivalries. But you won't be long like that, brothers, for these are the fires of God you've come to—these are the fires of God. A fig for your feuds and vendettas! Germans and Frenchmen, Irishmen and Englishmen, Jews and Russians—into the Crucible with you all! God is making the American.

MENDEL: I should have thought the American was made already—eighty millions of him.

DAVID: Eighty millions!

(*He smiles toward* VERA *in good-humoured derision*)

Eighty millions! Over a continent! Why, that cockleshell of a Britain has forty millions! No, uncle, the real American has not yet arrived. He is only in the Crucible, I tell you—he will be the fusion of all races, perhaps the coming superman. Ah, what a glorious Finale for my symphony—if I can only write it.

VERA: But you have written some of it already! May I not see it?

DAVID (*Relapsing into boyish shyness*): No, if you please, don't ask—

(*He moves over to his desk and nervously shuts it down and turns the keys of drawers as though protecting his* Ms)

VERA: Won't you give a bit of it at our Concert?

DAVID: Oh, it needs an orchestra.

VERA: But you at the violin and I at the piano—

MENDEL: You didn't tell me you played, Miss Revendal!

VERA: I told you less commonplace things.

DAVID: Miss Revendal plays quite like a professional.

VERA (*Smiling*): I don't feel so complimented as you expect. You see I did have a professional training.

MENDEL (*Smiling*): And I thought you came to *me* for lessons!

(DAVID *laughs*)

VERA (*Smiling*): No, I went to Petersburg—

DAVID (*Dazed*): To Petersburg—?

VERA (*Smiling*): Naturally. To the Conservatoire. There wasn't much music to be had at Kishineff, a town where—

DAVID: Kishineff!

(*He begins to tremble*)

VERA (*Still smiling*): My birthplace.

MENDEL (*Coming toward him, protectingly*): Calm yourself, David.

DAVID: Yes, yes—so you are a Russian!

(*He shudders violently, staggers*)

VERA (*Alarmed*): You are ill!

DAVID: It is nothing, I—not much music at Kishineff! No, only the Death-March! . . . Mother! Father! Ah—cowards, murderers! And you!

(*He shakes his fist at the air*)

You, looking on with your cold butcher's face! O God! O God!

(*He bursts into hysterical sobs and runs, shamefacedly, through the door to his room*)

VERA (*Wildly*): What have I said? What have I done?

MENDEL: Oh, I was afraid of this, I was afraid of this.

FRAU QUIXANO (*Who has fallen asleep over her book, wakes as if with a sense of the horror and gazes dazedly around, adding to the thrillingness of the moment*): Dovidel! Wu is' Dovidel! Mir dacht sach—

MENDEL (*Pressing her back to her slumbers*): Du träumst, Mutter! Schlaf!

(*She sinks back to sleep*)

VERA (*In hoarse whisper*): His father and mother were massacred?

MENDEL (*In same tense tone*): Before his eyes—father, mother, sisters, down to the youngest babe, whose skull was battered in by a hooligan's heel.

VERA: How did *he* escape?

MENDEL: He was shot in the shoulder, and fell unconscious. As he wasn't a girl, the hooligans left him for dead and hurried to fresh sport.

VERA: Terrible! Terrible!

(*Almost in tears*)

MENDEL (*Shrugging shoulders, hopelessly*): It is only Jewish history! . . . David belongs to the species of *pogrom* orphan—they arrive in the States by almost every ship.

VERA: Poor boy! Poor boy! And he looked so happy!

(*She half sobs*)

MENDEL: So he is, most of the time—a sunbeam took human shape when he was born. But naturally that dreadful scene left a scar on his brain, as the bullet left a scar on his shoulder, and he is always liable to see red when Kishineff is mentioned.

VERA: I will never mention my miserable birthplace to him again.

MENDEL: But you see every few months the newspapers tell us of another *pogrom*, and then he screams out against what he calls that butcher's face, so that I tremble for his reason. I tremble even when I see him writing that crazy music about America, for it only means he is brooding over the difference between America and Russia.

VERA: But perhaps—perhaps—all the terrible memory will pass peacefully away in his music.

MENDEL: There will always be the scar on his shoulder to remind him—whenever the wound twinges, it brings up these terrible faces and visions.

VERA: Is it on his right shoulder?

MENDEL: No—on his left. For a violinist that is even worse.

VERA: Ah, of course—the weight and the fingering.

(*Subconsciously placing and fingering an imaginary violin*)

MENDEL: That is why I fear so for his future—he will never be strong enough for the feats of bravura that the public demands.

VERA: The wild beasts! I feel more ashamed of my country than ever. But there's his symphony.

MENDEL: And who will look at that amateurish stuff? He knows so little of harmony and counterpoint—he breaks all the rules. I've tried to give him a few pointers—but he ought to have gone to Germany.

VERA: Perhaps it's not too late.

MENDEL (*Passionately*): Ah, if you and your friends could help him! See—I'm begging after all.

But it's not for myself.

VERA: My father loves music. Perhaps *he*—but no! he lives in Kishineff. But I will think—there are people here—I will write to you.

MENDEL (*Fervently*): Thank you! Thank you!

VERA: Now you must go to him. Good-bye. Tell him I count upon him for the Concert.

MENDEL: How good you are!

(*He follows her to the street-door*)

VERA (*At door*): Say good-bye for me to your mother—she seems asleep.

MENDEL (*Opening outer door*): I am sorry it is snowing so.

VERA: We Russians are used to it.

(*Smiling, at exit*)

Good-bye—let us hope your David will turn out a Rubinstein.

MENDEL (*Closing the doors softly*): I never thought a Russian Christian could be so human.

(*He looks at the clock*)

*Gott in Himmel*—my dancing class!

(*He hurries into the overcoat hanging on the hat-rack. Re-enter* DAVID, *having composed himself, but still somewhat dazed*)

DAVID: She is gone? Oh, but I have driven her away by my craziness. Is she very angry?

MENDEL: Quite the contrary—she expects you at the Concert, and what is more—

DAVID (*Ecstatically*): And she understood! She understood my Crucible of God! Oh, uncle, you don't know what it means to me to have somebody who understands me. Even you have never understood—

MENDEL (*Wounded*): Nonsense! How can Miss Revendal understand you better than your own uncle?

DAVID (*Mystically exalted*): I can't explain—I feel it.

MENDEL: Of course she's interested in your music, thank Heaven. But what true understanding can there be between a Russian Jew and a Russian Christian?

DAVID: What understanding? Aren't we both Americans?

MENDEL: Well, I haven't time to discuss it now.

(*He winds his muffler round his throat*)

DAVID: Why, where are you going?

MENDEL (*Ironically*): Where *should* I be going—in the snow—on the eve of the Sabbath? Suppose we say to synagogue!

DAVID: Oh, uncle—how you always seem to hanker after those old things!

MENDEL (*Tartly*): Nonsense!

(*He takes his umbrella from the stand*)

I don't like to see our people going to pieces, that's all.

DAVID: Then why did you come to America? Why didn't you work for a Jewish land? You're not even a Zionist.

MENDEL: I can't argue now. There's a pack of giggling schoolgirls waiting to waltz.

DAVID: The fresh romping young things! Think of their happiness! I should love to play for them.

MENDEL (*Sarcastically*): I can see you are yourself again.

(*He opens the street-door—turns back*)

What about your own lesson? Can't we go together?

DAVID: I must first write down what is singing in my soul—oh, uncle, it seems as if I knew suddenly what was wanting in my music!

MENDEL (*Drily*): Well, don't forget what is wanting in the house! The rent isn't paid yet.

(*Exit through street-door. As he goes out, he touches and kisses the* Mezuzah *on the door-post, with a subconsciously antagonistic revival of religious impulse.* DAVID *opens his desk, takes out a pile of musical manuscript, sprawls over his chair and, humming to himself, scribbles feverishly with the quill. After a few moments* FRAU QUIXANO *yawns, wakes, and stretches herself. Then she looks at the clock*)

FRAU QUIXANO: *Shabbos!*

(*She rises and goes to the table and sees there are no candles, walks to the chiffonier and gets them and places them in the candlesticks, then lights the candles, muttering a ceremonial Hebrew benediction*)

Boruch atto haddoshem ellôheinu melech hoôlam assher kiddishonu bemitzvôsov vettzivonu lehadlik neir shel shabbos.

(*She pulls down the blinds of the two windows, then she goes to the rapt composer and touches him, remindingly, on the shoulder. He does not move, but continues writing*)

Dovidel!

(*He looks up dazedly. She points to the candles*)
   Shabbos!
(*A sweet smile comes over his face, he throws the quill resignedly away and submits his head to her hands and her muttered Hebrew blessing*)
   Yesimcho elôhim ke-efrayim vechimnasseh—yevorechecho haddoshem veyishmerecho, yoer hadoshem ponov eilecho vechunecho, yisso hadoshem ponov eilecho veyosem lecho sholôm.
(*Then she goes toward the kitchen. As she turns at the door, he is again writing. She shakes her finger at him, repeating*)
   Gut Shabbos!

DAVID: *Gut Shabbos!*

(*Puts down the pen and smiles after her till the door closes, then with a deep sigh takes his cape from the peg and his violin-case, pauses, still humming, to take up his pen and write down a fresh phrase, finally puts on his hat and is just about to open the street-door when* KATHLEEN *enters from her bedroom fully dressed to go, and laden with a large brown paper parcel and an umbrella. He turns at the sound of her footsteps and remains at the door, holding his violin-case during the ensuing dialogue*)

DAVID: You're not going out this bitter weather?

KATHLEEN (*Sharply fending him off with her umbrella*): And who's to shtay me?

DAVID: Oh, but you mustn't—*I'll* do your errand—what is it?

KATHLEEN (*Indignantly*): Errand, is it, indeed! I'm not here!

DAVID: Not here?

KATHLEEN: I'm lavin', they'll come for me thrunk—and ye'll witness I don't take the candleshtick.

DAVID: But who's sending you away?

KATHLEEN: It's sending meself away I am—yer houly grandmother has me disthroyed intirely.

DAVID: Why, what has the poor old la—?

KATHLEEN: I don't be saltin' the mate and I do be mixin' the crockery and—!

DAVID (*Gently*): I know, I know—but, Kathleen, remember she was brought up to these things from childhood. And her father was a Rabbi.

KATHLEEN: What's that? A priest?

DAVID: A sort of priest. In Russia he was a great man. Her husband, too, was a mighty scholar, and to give him time to study the holy books she had to do chores all day for him and the children.

KATHLEEN: Oh, those priests!

DAVID (*Smiling*): No, *he* wasn't a priest. But he took sick and died and the children left her—went to America or heaven or other far-off places—and she was left all penniless and alone.

KATHLEEN: Poor ould lady.

DAVID: Not so old yet, for she was married at fifteen.

KATHLEEN: Poor young crathur!

DAVID: But she was still the good angel of the congregation—sat up with the sick and watched over the dead.

KATHLEEN: Saints alive! And not scared?

DAVID: No, nothing scared her—except me. I got a broken-down fiddle and used to play it even on *Shabbos*—I was very naughty. But she was so lovely to me. I still remember the heavenly taste of a piece of *Motso* she gave me dipped in raisin wine! Passover cake, you know.

KATHLEEN (*Proudly*): Oh, I know *Motso*.

DAVID (*Smacks his lips, repeats*): Heavenly!

KATHLEEN: Sure, I must tashte it.

DAVID (*Shaking his head, mysteriously*): Only little boys get that tashte.

KATHLEEN: That's quare.

DAVID (*Smiling*): Very quare. And then one day my uncle sent the old lady a ticket to come to America. But it is not so happy for her here because you see my uncle has to be near his theatre and can't live in the Jewish quarter, and so nobody understands her, and she sits all the livelong day alone—alone with her book and her religion and her memories—

KATHLEEN (*Breaking down*): Oh, Mr. David!

DAVID: And now all this long, cold, snowy evening she'll sit by the fire alone, thinking of her dead, and the fire will sink lower and lower, and she won't be able to touch it, because it's the holy Sabbath, and there'll be no kind Kathleen to brighten up the grey ashes, and then at last, sad and shivering, she'll creep up to her room without a candlestick, and there in the dark and the cold—

KATHLEEN (*Hysterically bursting into tears, dropping her parcel, and untying her bonnet-strings*): Oh, Mr. David, I won't mix the crockery, I won't—

DAVID (*Heartily*): Of course you won't. Good night.

(*He slips out hurriedly through the street-door as* KATHLEEN *throws off her bonnet, and the curtain falls quickly. As it rises again, she is seen strenuously poking the fire, illumined by its red glow*)

## Act II

*The same scene on an afternoon a month later.* DAVID *is discovered at his desk, scribbling music in a fever of enthusiasm.* MENDEL, *dressed in his best, is playing softly on the piano, watching* DAVID. *After an instant or two of indecision, he puts down the piano-lid with a bang and rises decisively.*

MENDEL: David!

DAVID (*Putting up his left hand*): Please, please—

(*He writes feverishly*)

MENDEL: But I want to talk to you seriously—at once.

DAVID: I'm just re-writing the Finale. Oh, such a splendid inspiration!

(*He writes on*)

MENDEL (*Shrugs his shoulders and reseats himself at piano. He plays a bar or two. Looks at watch impatiently. Resolutely*): David, I've got wonderful news for you. Miss Revendal is bringing somebody to see you, and we have hopes of getting you sent to Germany to study composition.

(DAVID *does not reply, but writes rapidly on*)

Why, he hasn't heard a word!

(*He shouts*)

David!

DAVID (*Writing on*): I can't, uncle. I *must* put it down while that glorious impression is fresh.

MENDEL: What impression? You only went to the People's Alliance.

DAVID: Yes, and there I saw the Jewish children—a thousand of 'em— saluting the Flag.

(*He writes on*)

MENDEL: Well, what of that?

DAVID: What of that?

(*He throws down his quill and jumps up*)

But just fancy it, uncle. The Stars and Stripes unfurled, and a thousand childish voices, piping and foreign, fresh from the lands of oppression, hailing its fluttering folds. I cried like a baby.

MENDEL: I'm afraid you *are* one.

DAVID: Ah, but if you had heard them—"Flag of our Great Republic"—the words have gone singing at my heart ever since—

(*He turns to the flag over the door*)

"Flag of our Great Republic, guardian of our homes, whose stars and stripes stand for Bravery, Purity, Truth, and Union, we salute thee. We, the natives of distant lands, who find

(*Half-sobbing*)

rest under thy folds, do pledge our hearts, our lives, our sacred honour to love and protect thee, our Country, and the liberty of the American people for ever."

(*He ends almost hysterically*)

MENDEL (*Soothingly*): Quite right. But you needn't get so excited over it.

DAVID: Not when one hears the roaring of the fires of God? Not when one sees the souls melting in the Crucible? Uncle, all those little Jews will grow up Americans!

MENDEL (*Putting a pacifying hand on his shoulder and forcing him into a chair*): Sit down. I want to talk to you about your affairs.

DAVID (*Sitting*): *My* affairs! But I've been talking about them all the time!

MENDEL: Nonsense, David.

(*He sits beside him*)

Don't you think it's time you got into a wider world?

DAVID: Eh? This planet's wide enough for me.

MENDEL: Do be serious. You don't want to live all your life in this room.

DAVID (*Looks round*): What's the matter with this room? It's princely.

MENDEL (*Raising his hands in horror*): Princely!

DAVID: Imperial. Remember when I first saw it—after pigging a week in the rocking steerage, swinging in a berth as wide as my fiddle-case, hung near the cooking-engines; imagine the hot rancid smell of the food, the oil of the machinery, the odours of all that close-packed, sea-sick—

MENDEL (*Putting his hand over DAVID's mouth*): Don't! You make me ill! How could you ever bear it?

DAVID (*Smiling*): I was quite happy—I only had to fancy I'd been shipwrecked, and that after clinging to a plank five days without food or water on the great lonely Atlantic, my frozen, sodden form had been picked up by this great safe steamer and given this delightful dry berth, regular meals, and the spectacle of all these friendly faces. . . Do you know who was on board that boat? Quincy Davenport.

MENDEL: The lord of corn and oil?

DAVID (*Smiling*): Yes, even we wretches in the steerage felt safe to think the lord was up above, we believed the company would never dare drown *him*. But could even Quincy Davenport command a cabin like this?

(*Waving his arm round the room*)

Why, uncle, we have a cabin worth a thousand dollars—a thousand dollars a *week*—and what's more, it doesn't wobble!

(*He plants his feet voluptuously upon the floor*)

MENDEL: Come, come, David, I asked you to be serious. Surely, some day you'd like your music produced?

DAVID (*Jumps up*): Wouldn't it be glorious? To hear it all actually coming out of violins and 'cellos, drums and trumpets.

MENDEL: And you'd like it to go all over the world?

DAVID: All over the world and all down the ages.

MENDEL: But don't you see that unless you go and study seriously in Germany—?

(*Enter* KATHLEEN *from kitchen, carrying a furnished tea-tray with ear-shaped cakes, bread and butter, etc., and wearing a grotesque false nose.* MENDEL *cries out in amaze*)

Kathleen!

DAVID (*Roaring with boyish laughter*): Ha! Ha! Ha! Ha! Ha!

KATHLEEN (*Standing still with her tray*): Sure, what's the matter?

DAVID: Look in the glass!

KATHLEEN (*Going to the mantel*): Houly Moses!

(*She drops the tray, which* MENDEL *catches, and snatches off the nose*)

Och, I forgot to take it off—'twas the misthress gave it me—I put it on to cheer her up.

DAVID: Is she so miserable, then?

KATHLEEN: Terrible low, Mr. David, to-day being *Purim*.

MENDEL: *Purim!* Is to-day *Purim*?

(*Gives her the tea-tray back.* KATHLEEN, *to take it, drops her nose and forgets to pick it up*)

DAVID: But *Purim* is a merry time, Kathleen, like your Carnival. Haven't you read the book of Esther—how the Jews of Persia escaped massacre?

KATHLEEN: That's what the misthress is so miserable about. Ye don't *keep* the Carnival. There's noses for both of ye in the kitchen— didn't I go with her to Hester Street to buy 'em?—but ye don't be axin' for 'em. And to see your noses layin' around so solemn and neglected, faith, it nearly makes me chry meself.

MENDEL (*Bitterly to himself*): Who can remember about *Purim* in America?

DAVID (*Half-smiling*): Poor granny, tell her to come in and I'll play her *Purim* jig.

MENDEL (*Hastily*): No, no, David, not here—the visitors!

DAVID: Visitors? What visitors?

MENDEL (*Impatiently*): That's just what I've been trying to explain.

DAVID: Well, I can play in the kitchen.

(*He takes his violin. Exit to kitchen.* MENDEL *sighs and shrugs his shoulders hopelessly at the boy's perversity, then fingers the cups and saucers*)

MENDEL (*Anxiously*): Is that the *best* tea-set?

KATHLEEN: Can't you see it's the Passover set!

(*Ruefully*)

And shpiled intirely it'll be now for our Passover. . . And the misthress thought the visitors might like to thry some of her *Purim* cakes.

(*Indicates ear-shaped cakes on tray*)

MENDEL (*Bitterly*): *Purim* cakes!

(*He turns his back on her and stares moodily out of the window*)

KATHLEEN (*Mutters contemptuously*): Call yerself a Jew and you forgettin' to keep *Purim*!

(*She is going back to the kitchen when a merry Slavic dance breaks out, softened by the door; her feet unconsciously get more and more into dance step, and at last she jigs out. As she opens and passes through the door, the music sounds louder*)

FRAU QUIXANO (*Heard from kitchen*): Ha! Ha! Ha! Ha! Ha! Kathleen!!

(MENDEL'S *feet, too, begin to take the swing of the music, and his feet dance as he stares out of the window. Suddenly the hoot of an automobile is heard, followed by the rattling up of the car*)

MENDEL: Ah, she has brought somebody swell!

(*He throws open the doors and goes out eagerly to meet the visitors. The dance music goes on softly throughout the scene*)

QUINCY DAVENPORT (*Outside*): Oh, thank you—I leave the coats in the car.

(*Enter an instant later* QUINCY DAVENPORT *and* VERA REVENDAL, MENDEL *in the rear.* VERA *is dressed much as before, but with a motor veil, which she takes off during the scene.* DAVENPORT *is a dude, aping the air of a European sporting clubman. Aged about thirty-five and well set-up, he wears an orchid and an intermittent eyeglass, and gives the impression of a coarse-fibred and patronisingly facetious but not bad-hearted man, spoiled by prosperity)*

MENDEL: Won't you be seated?

VERA: First let me introduce my friend, who is good enough to interest himself in your nephew—Mr. Quincy Davenport.

MENDEL (*Struck of a heap*): Mr. Quincy Davenport! How strange!

VERA: What is strange?

MENDEL: David just mentioned Mr. Davenport's name—said they travelled to New York on the same boat.

QUINCY: Impossible! Always travel on my own yacht. Slow but select. Must have been another man of the same name—my dad. Ha! Ha! Ha!

MENDEL: Ah, of course. I thought you were too young.

QUINCY: My dad, Miss Revendal, is one of those antiquated Americans who are always in a hurry!

VERA: He burns coal and you burn time.

QUINCY: Precisely! Ha! Ha! Ha!

MENDEL: Won't you sit down—I'll go and prepare David.

VERA (*Sitting*): You've not prepared him yet?

MENDEL: I've tried to more than once—but I never really got to— (*He smiles*)

to Germany.

(QUINCY *sits*)

VERA: Then prepare him for *three* visitors.

MENDEL: Three?

VERA: You see Mr. Davenport himself is no judge of music.

QUINCY (*Jumps up*): I beg your pardon.

VERA: In manuscript.

QUINCY: Ah, of course not. Music should be heard, not seen—like that jolly jig. Is that your David?

MENDEL: Oh, you mustn't judge him by that. He's just fooling.

QUINCY: Oh, he'd better not fool with Poppy. Poppy's awful severe.

MENDEL: Poppy?

QUINCY: Pappelmeister—my private orchestra conductor.

MENDEL: Is it *your* orchestra Pappelmeister conducts?

QUINCY: Well, I pay the piper—and the drummer too! (*He chuckles*)

MENDEL (*Sadly*): *I* wanted to play in it, but he turned me down.

QUINCY: I told you he was awful severe.

(*To* VERA)

He only allows me comic opera once a week. My wife calls him the Bismarck of the baton.

MENDEL (*Reverently*): A great conductor!

QUINCY: Would he have a twenty-thousand-dollar job with me if he wasn't? Not that he'd get half that in the open market—only I have to stick it on to keep him for my guests exclusively.

(*Looks at watch*)

But he ought to be here, confound him. A conductor should keep time, eh, Miss Revendal?

(*He sniggers*)

MENDEL: I'll bring David. Won't you help yourselves to tea?

(*To* VERA)

You see there's lemon for you—as in Russia.

(*Exit to kitchen—a moment afterwards the merry music stops in the middle of a bar*)

VERA: Thank you.

(*Taking a cup*)

Do *you* like lemon, Mr. Davenport?

QUINCY (*Flirtatiously*): That depends. The last I had was in Russia itself—from the fair hands of your mother, the Baroness.

VERA (*Pained*): Please don't say my mother, my mother is dead.

QUINCY (*Fatuously misunderstanding*): Oh, you have no call to be ashamed of your step-mother—she's a stunning creature; all the points of a tip-top Russian aristocrat, or Quincy Davenport's no judge of breed! Doesn't speak English like your father—but then the Baron is a wonder.

VERA (*Takes up teapot*): Father once hoped to be British Ambassador—that's why *I* had an English governess. But you never told me you met him in *Russia*.

QUINCY: Surely! When I gave you all those love messages—

VERA (*Pouring tea quickly*): You said you met him at Wiesbaden.

QUINCY: Yes, but we grew such pals I motored him and the Baroness back to St. Petersburg. Jolly country, Russia—they know how to live.

VERA (*Coldly*): I saw more of those who know how to die. . . Milk and sugar?

QUINCY (*Sentimentally*): Oh, Miss Revendal! Have you forgotten?

VERA (*Politely snubbing*): How should I remember?

QUINCY: You don't remember our first meeting? At the Settlement Bazaar? When I paid you a hundred dollars for every piece of sugar you put in?

VERA: Did you? Then I hope you drank syrup.

QUINCY: Ugh! I hate sugar—I sacrificed myself.

VERA: To the Settlement? How heroic of you!

QUINCY: No, not to the Settlement. To you!

VERA: Then I'll only put milk in.

QUINCY: I hate milk. But from you—

VERA: Then we *must* fall back on the lemon.

QUINCY: I loathe lemon. But from—

VERA: Then you shall have your tea neat.

QUINCY: I detest tea, and here it would be particularly cheap and nasty. But—

VERA: Then you shall have a cake!

(*She offers plate*)

QUINCY (*Taking one*): Would they be eatable?

(*Tasting it*)

Humph! Not bad.

(*Sentimentally*)

A little cake was all you would eat the only time you came to one of my private concerts. Don't you remember? We went down to supper together.

VERA (*Taking his tea for herself and putting in lemon*): I shall always remember the delicious music Herr Pappelmeister gave us.

QUINCY: How unkind of you!

VERA: Unkind?

(*She sips the tea and puts down the cup*)

To be grateful for the music?

QUINCY: You know what I mean—to forget *me*!

(*He tries to take her hand*)

VERA (*Rising*): Aren't you forgetting yourself?

QUINCY: You mean because I'm married to that patched-and-painted creature? She's hankering for the stage again, the old witch.

VERA: Hush! Marriages with comic opera stars are not usually domestic idylls.

QUINCY: I fell a victim to my love of music.

VERA (*Murmurs, smiling*): Music!

QUINCY: And I hadn't yet met the right breed—the true blue blood of Europe. I'll get a divorce.

(*Approaching her*)

Vera!

VERA (*Retreating*): You will make me sorry I came to you.

QUINCY: No, don't say that—promised the Baron I'd always do all I could for—

VERA: You promised? You dared discuss my affairs?

QUINCY: It was your father began it. When he found I knew you, he almost wept with emotion. He asked a hundred questions about your life in America.

VERA: His life and mine are for ever separate. He is a Reactionary, I a Radical.

QUINCY: But he loves you dreadfully—he can't understand why you should go slaving away summer and winter in a Settlement—you a member of the Russian nobility!

VERA (*With faint smile*): I might say, *noblesse oblige*. But the truth is, I earn my living that way. It would do *you* good to slave there too!

QUINCY (*Eagerly*): Would they chain us together? I'd come to-morrow.

(*He moves nearer her. There is a double knock at the door*)

VERA (*Relieved*): Here's Pappelmeister!

QUINCY: Bother Poppy—why is he so darned punctual?

(*Enter* KATHLEEN *from the kitchen*)

VERA (*Smiling*): Ah, you're still here.

KATHLEEN: And why would I not be here?

(*She goes to open the door*)

PAPPELMEISTER: Mr. Quixano?

KATHLEEN: Yes, come in.

(*Enter* HERR PAPPELMEISTER, *a burly German figure with a leonine head, spectacles, and a mane of white hair—a figure that makes his employer look even coarser. He carries an umbrella, which he never lets go. He is at first grave and silent, which makes any burst of emotion the more striking. He and* QUINCY DAVENPORT *suggest a picture of "Dignity and Impudence." His English, as roughly indicated in the text, is extremely Teutonic*)

QUINCY: You're late, Poppy!

(PAPPELMEISTER *silently bows to* VERA)

VERA (*Smilingly goes and offers her hand*): Proud to meet you, Herr Pappelmeister!

QUINCY: Excuse me—

*(Introducing)*

Miss Revendal!—I forgot you and Poppy hadn't been introduced—curiously enough it was at Wiesbaden I picked him up too—he was conducting the opera—your folks were in my box. I don't think I ever met anyone so mad on music as the Baron. And the Baroness told me he had retired from active service in the Army because of the torture of listening to the average military band. Ha! Ha! Ha!

VERA: Yes, my father once hoped *my* music would comfort him.

*(She smiles sadly)*

Poor father! But a soldier must bear defeat. Herr Pappelmeister, may I not give you some tea?

*(She sits again at the table)*

QUINCY: Tea! Lager's more in Poppy's line.

*(He chuckles)*

PAPPELMEISTER *(Gravely)*: *Bitte*. Tea.

*(She pours out, he sits)*

Lemon. Four lumps. . . *Nun*, five! . . . Or six!

*(She hands him the cup)*

Danke.

*(As he receives the cup, he utters an exclamation, for* KATHLEEN *after opening the door has lingered on, hunting around everywhere, and having finally crawled under the table has now brushed against his leg)*

VERA: What are you looking for?

KATHLEEN *(Her head emerging)*: My nose!

*(They are all startled and amused)*

VERA: Your nose?

KATHLEEN: I forgot me nose!

QUINCY: Well, follow your nose—and you'll find it. Ha! Ha! Ha!

KATHLEEN *(Pouncing on it)*: Here it is!

*(Picks it up near the armchair)*

OMNES: Oh!

KATHLEEN: Sure, it's gotten all dirthy.

*(She takes out a handkerchief and wipes the nose carefully)*

QUINCY: But why do you want a nose like that?

KATHLEEN *(Proudly)*: Bekaz we're Hebrews!

QUINCY: What!

VERA: What *do* you mean?

KATHLEEN: It's our Carnival to-day! *Purim.*

(*She carries her nose carefully and piously toward the kitchen*)

VERA: Oh! I see.

(*Exit* KATHLEEN)

QUINCY (*In horror*): Miss Revendal, you don't mean to say you've brought me to a Jew!

VERA: I'm afraid I have. I was thinking only of his genius, not his race. And you see, so many musicians are Jews.

QUINCY: Not *my* musicians. No Jew's harp in my orchestra, eh?

(*He sniggers*)

I wouldn't have a Jew if he paid *me*.

VERA: I daresay you have some, all the same.

QUINCY: Impossible. Poppy! Are there any Jews in my orchestra?

PAPPELMEISTER (*Removing the cup from his mouth and speaking with sepulchral solemnity*): Do you mean are dere any Christians?

QUINCY (*In horror*): Gee-rusalem! Perhaps *you're* a Jew!

PAPPELMEISTER (*Gravely*): I haf not de honour. But, if you brefer, I will gut out from all de brogrammes all de Chewish composers. *Was?*

QUINCY: Why, of course. Fire 'em out, every mother's son of 'em.

PAPPELMEISTER (*Unsmiling*): *Also*—no more comic operas!

QUINCY: What!!!

PAPPELMEISTER: Dey write all de comic operas!

QUINCY: Brute!

(PAPPELMEISTER'*s chuckle is heard gurgling in his cup. Re-enter* MENDEL *from kitchen*)

MENDEL (*To* VERA): I'm so sorry—I can't get him to come in—he's terrible shy.

QUINCY: Won't face the music, eh?

(*He sniggers*)

VERA: Did you tell him *I* was here?

MENDEL: Of course.

VERA (*Disappointed*): Oh!

MENDEL: But I've persuaded him to let me show his Ms.

VERA (*With forced satisfaction*): Oh, well, that's all we want.

(MENDEL *goes to the desk, opens it, and gets the* Ms. *and offers it to* QUINCY DAVENPORT)

QUINCY: Not for me—Poppy!

(MENDEL *offers it to* PAPPELMEISTER, *who takes it solemnly*)

MENDEL (*Anxiously to* PAPPELMEISTER): Of course you must remember his youth and his lack of musical education—

PAPPELMEISTER: *Bitte, das Pult!*

(MENDEL *moves* DAVID'S *music-stand from the corner to the centre of the room.* PAPPELMEISTER *puts Ms. on it*)

*So!*

(*All eyes centre on him eagerly,* MENDEL *standing uneasily, the others sitting.* PAPPELMEISTER *polishes his glasses with irritating elaborateness and weary* "*achs,*" *then reads in absolute silence. A pause*)

QUINCY (*Bored by the silence*): But won't you play it to us?

PAPPELMEISTER: Blay it? Am I an orchestra? I blay it in my brain.

(*He goes on reading, his brow gets wrinkled. He ruffles his hair unconsciously. All watch him anxiously—he turns the page*)

*So!*

VERA (*Anxiously*): You don't seem to like it!

PAPPELMEISTER: I do not comprehend it.

MENDEL: I knew it was crazy—it is supposed to be about America or a Crucible or something. And of course there are heaps of mistakes.

VERA: That is why I am suggesting to Mr. Davenport to send him to Germany.

QUINCY: I'll send as many Jews as you like to Germany. Ha! Ha! Ha!

PAPPELMEISTER (*Absorbed, turning pages*): *Ach!—ach!—So!*

QUINCY: I'd even lend my own yacht to take 'em back. Ha! Ha! Ha!

VERA: Sh! We're disturbing Herr Pappelmeister.

QUINCY: Oh, Poppy's all right.

PAPPELMEISTER (*Sublimely unconscious*): *Ach so—so—So! Das ist etwas neues!*

(*His umbrella begins to beat time, moving more and more vigorously, till at last he is conducting elaborately, stretching out his left palm for pianissimo passages, and raising it vigorously for forte, with every now and then an exclamation*)

*Wunderschön!* . . . *pianissimo!*—now the flutes! Clarinets! *Ach, ergötzlich.* . . bassoons and drums! . . . *Fortissimo!* . . . *Kolossal! Kolossal!*

(*Conducting in a fury of enthusiasm*)

VERA (*Clapping her hands*): Bravo! Bravo! I'm so excited!

QUINCY (*Yawning*): Then it isn't bad, Poppy?

PAPPELMEISTER (*Not listening, never ceasing to conduct*): *Und* de harp solo. . . *ach, reizend!* . . . Second violins—!

QUINCY: But Poppy! We can't be here all day.

PAPPELMEISTER (*Not listening, continuing pantomime action*): Sh! Sh! Piano.

ISRAEL ZANGWILL

QUINCY (*Outraged*): Sh to *me*!
(*Rises*)

VERA: He doesn't know it's you.

QUINCY: But look here, Poppy—

(*He seizes the wildly-moving umbrella. Blank stare of* PAPPELMEISTER *gradually returning to consciousness*)

PAPPELMEISTER: *Was giebt's. . . ?*

QUINCY: We've had enough.

PAPPELMEISTER (*Indignant*): Enough? Enough? Of such a beaudiful symphony?

QUINCY: It may be beautiful to you, but to us it's damn dull. See here, Poppy, if you're satisfied that the young fellow has sufficient talent to be sent to study in Germany—

PAPPELMEISTER: In Germany! Germany has nodings to teach him, he has to teach Germany.

VERA: Bravo!

(*She springs up*)

MENDEL: I always said he was a genius!

QUINCY: Well, at that rate you could put this stuff of his in one of my programmes. *Sinfonia Americana*, eh?

VERA: Oh, that *is* good of you.

PAPPELMEISTER: I should be broud to indroduce it to de vorld.

VERA: And will it be played in that wonderful marble music-room overlooking the Hudson?

QUINCY: Sure. Before five hundred of the smartest folk in America.

MENDEL: Oh, thank you, thank you. That will mean fame!

QUINCY: And dollars. Don't forget the dollars.

MENDEL: I'll run and tell him.

(*He hastens into the kitchen,* PAPPELMEISTER *is re-absorbed in the* Ms., *but no longer conducting*)

QUINCY: You see, I'll help even a Jew for your sake.

VERA: Hush!

(*Indicating* PAPPELMEISTER)

QUINCY: Oh, Poppy's in the moon.

VERA: You must help him for his own sake, for art's sake.

QUINCY: And why not for heart's sake—for my sake?

(*He comes nearer*)

VERA (*Crossing to* PAPPELMEISTER): Herr Pappelmeister! When do you think you can produce it?

PAPPELMEISTER: *Wunderbar!* . . .
(*Becoming half-conscious of* VERA)
    Four lumps. . .
(*Waking up*)
    *Bitte?*
VERA: How soon can you produce it?
PAPPELMEISTER: How soon can he finish it?
VERA: Isn't it finished?
PAPPELMEISTER: I see von Finale scratched out and anoder not quite
    completed. But anyhow, ve couldn't broduce it before Saturday
    fortnight.
QUINCY: Saturday fortnight! Not time to get my crowd.
PAPPELMEISTER: Den ve say Saturday dree veeks. Yes?
QUINCY: Yes. Stop a minute! Did you say Saturday? That's my comic
    opera night! You thief!
PAPPELMEISTER: Somedings must be sagrificed.
MENDEL (*Outside*): But you *must* come, David.
(*The kitchen door opens, and* MENDEL *drags in the boyishly shrinking*
DAVID. PAPPELMEISTER *thumps with his umbrella,* VERA *claps her hands,*
QUINCY DAVENPORT *produces his eyeglass and surveys* DAVID *curiously*)
VERA: Oh, Mr. Quixano, I am so glad! Mr. Davenport is going to
    produce your symphony in his wonderful music-room.
QUINCY: Yes, young man, I'm going to give you the smartest audience
    in America. And if Poppy is right, you're just going to rake in the
    dollars. America wants a composer.
PAPPELMEISTER (*Raises hands emphatically*): *Ach Gott, ja!*
VERA (*To* DAVID): Why don't you speak? You're not angry with me for
    interfering—?
DAVID: I can never be grateful enough to you—
VERA: Oh, not to me. It is to Mr. Davenport you—
DAVID: And I can never be grateful enough to Herr Pappelmeister. It
    is an honour even to meet him.
(*Bows*)
PAPPELMEISTER (*Choking with emotion, goes and pats him on the back*):
    *Mein braver Junge!*
VERA (*Anxiously*): But it is Mr. Davenport—
DAVID: Before I accept Mr. Davenport's kindness, I must know
    to whom I am indebted—and if Mr. Davenport is the man
    who—

QUINCY: Who travelled with you to New York? Ha! Ha! Ha! No, *I'm* only the junior.

DAVID: Oh, I know, sir, you don't make the money you spend.

QUINCY: Eh?

VERA (*Anxiously*): He means he knows you're not in business.

DAVID: Yes, sir; but is it true you are in pleasure?

QUINCY (*Puzzled*): I beg your pardon?

DAVID: Are all the stories the papers print about you true?

QUINCY: *All* the stories. That's a tall order. Ha! Ha! Ha!

DAVID: Well, anyhow, is it true that—?

VERA: Mr. Quixano! What *are* you driving at?

QUINCY: Oh, it's rather fun to hear what the masses read about me. Fire ahead. Is what true?

DAVID: That you were married in a balloon?

QUINCY: Ho! Ha! Ha! That's true enough. Marriage in high life, they said, didn't they? Ha! Ha! Ha!

DAVID: And is it true you live in America only two months in the year, and then only to entertain Europeans who wander to these wild parts?

QUINCY: Lucky for you, young man. You'll have an Italian prince and a British duke to hear your scribblings.

DAVID: And the palace where they will hear my scribblings—is it true that—?

VERA (*Who has been on pins and needles*): Mr. Quixano, what possible—?

DAVID (*Entreatingly holds up a hand*): Miss Revendal!
(*To* QUINCY DAVENPORT)
Is this palace the same whose grounds were turned into Venetian canals where the guests ate in gondolas—gondolas that were draped with the most wonderful trailing silks in imitation of the Venetian nobility in the great water fêtes?

QUINCY (*Turns to* VERA): Ah, Miss Revendal—what a pity you refused that invitation! It was a fairy scene of twinkling lights and delicious darkness—each couple had their own gondola to sup in, and their own side-canal to slip down. Eh? Ha! Ha! Ha!

DAVID: And the same night, women and children died of hunger in New York!

QUINCY (*Startled, drops eyeglass*): Eh?

DAVID (*Furiously*): And this is the sort of people you would invite to hear my symphony—these gondola-guzzlers!

VERA: Mr. Quixano!

MENDEL: David!

DAVID: These magnificent animals who went into the gondolas two by two, to feed and flirt!

QUINCY (*Dazed*): Sir!

DAVID: I should be a new freak for you for a new freak evening—I and my dreams and my music!

QUINCY: You low-down, ungrateful—

DAVID: Not for you and such as you have I sat here writing and dreaming; not for you who are killing my America!

QUINCY: *Your* America, forsooth, you Jew-immigrant!

VERA: Mr. Davenport!

DAVID: Yes—Jew-immigrant! But a Jew who knows that your Pilgrim Fathers came straight out of his Old Testament, and that our Jew-immigrants are a greater factor in the glory of this great commonwealth than some of you sons of the soil. It is you, freak-fashionables, who are undoing the work of Washington and Lincoln, vulgarising your high heritage, and turning the last and noblest hope of humanity into a caricature.

QUINCY (*Rocking with laughter*): Ha! Ha! Ha! Ho! Ho! Ho!

(*To* VERA)

You never told me your Jew-scribbler was a socialist!

DAVID: I am nothing but a simple artist, but I come from Europe, one of her victims, and I know that she is a failure; that her palaces and peerages are outworn toys of the human spirit, and that the only hope of mankind lies in a new world. And here—in the land of to-morrow—you are trying to bring back Europe—

QUINCY (*Interjecting*): I wish we could!—

DAVID: Europe with her comic-opera coronets and her worm-eaten stage decorations, and her pomp and chivalry built on a morass of crime and misery—

QUINCY (*With sneering laugh*): Morass!

DAVID (*With prophetic passion*): But you shall not kill my dream! There shall come a fire round the Crucible that will melt you and your breed like wax in a blowpipe—

QUINCY (*Furiously, with clenched fist*): You—

DAVID: America *shall* make good. . . !

PAPPELMEISTER (*Who has sat down and remained imperturbably seated throughout all this scene, springs up and waves his umbrella hysterically*): *Hoch Quixano! Hoch! Hoch! Es lebe Quixano! Hoch!*

QUINCY: Poppy! You're dismissed!

PAPPELMEISTER (*Goes to* DAVID *with outstretched hand*): *Danke.*

(*They grip hands.* PAPPELMEISTER *turns to* QUINCY DAVENPORT) Comic Opera! Ouf!

QUINCY (*Goes to street-door, at white heat*): Are you coming, Miss Revendal?

(*He opens the door*)

VERA (*To* QUINCY, *but not moving*): Pray, pray, accept my apologies— believe me, if I had known—

QUINCY (*Furiously*): Then stop with your Jew!

(*Exit*)

MENDEL (*Frantically*): But, Mr. Davenport—don't go! He is only a boy.

(*Exit after* QUINCY DAVENPORT) You must consider—

DAVID: Oh, Herr Pappelmeister, you have lost your place!

PAPPELMEISTER: And saved my soul. Dollars are de devil. Now I must to an appointment.

*Auf baldiges Wiedersehen.*

(*He shakes* DAVID's *hand*) Fräulein Revendal!

(*He takes her hand and kisses it. Exit.* DAVID *and* VERA *stand gazing at each other*)

VERA: What have you done? What have you done?

DAVID: What else could I do?

VERA: I hate the smart set as much as you—but as your ladder and your trumpet—

DAVID: I would not stand indebted to them. I know you meant it for my good, but what would these Europe-apers have understood of *my* America—the America of my music? They look back on Europe as a pleasure ground, a palace of art—but I know

(*Getting hysterical*) it is sodden with blood, red with bestial massacres—

VERA (*Alarmed, anxious*): Let us talk no more about it.

(*She holds out her hand*) Good-bye.

DAVID (*Frozen, taking it, holding it*): Ah, you are offended by my ingratitude—I shall never see you again.

VERA: No, I am not offended. But I have failed to help you. We have nothing else to meet for.

(*She disengages her hand*)

DAVID: Why will you punish me so? I have only hurt myself.

VERA: It is not a *punishment*.

DAVID: What else? When you are with me, all the air seems to tremble with fairy music played by some unseen fairy orchestra.

VERA (*Tremulous*): And yet you wouldn't come in just now when I—

DAVID: I was too frightened of the others. . .

VERA (*Smiling*): Frightened indeed!

DAVID: Yes, I know I became overbold—but to take all that magic sweetness out of my life for ever—you don't call that a punishment?

VERA (*Blushing*): How could I wish to punish you? I was proud of you!

(*Drops her eyes, murmurs*)

Besides it would be punishing *myself*.

DAVID (*In passionate amaze*): Miss Revendal! . . . But no, it cannot be. It is too impossible.

VERA (*Frightened*): Yes, too impossible. Good-bye.

(*She turns*)

DAVID: But not for always?

(VERA *hangs her head. He comes nearer. Passionately*)

Promise me that you—that I—

(*He takes her hand again*)

VERA (*Melting at his touch, breathes*): Yes, yes, David.

DAVID: Miss Revendal!

(*She falls into his arms*)

VERA: My dear! my dear!

DAVID: It is a dream. You cannot care for me—you so far above me.

VERA: Above you, you simple boy? Your genius lifts you to the stars.

DAVID: No, no; it is you who lift me there—

VERA (*Smoothing his hair*): Oh, David. And to think that I was brought up to despise your race.

DAVID (*Sadly*): Yes, all Russians are.

VERA: But we of the nobility in particular.

DAVID (*Amazed, half-releasing her*): You are noble?

VERA: My father is Baron Revendal, but I have long since carved out a life of my own.

DAVID: Then he will not separate us?

VERA: No.

(*Re-embracing him*)

Nothing can separate us.

(*A knock at the street-door. They separate. The automobile is heard clattering off*)

DAVID: It is my uncle coming back.

VERA (*In low, tense tones*): Then I shall slip out. I could not bear a third. I will write.

(*She goes to the door*)

DAVID: Yes, yes. . . Vera.

(*He follows her to the door. He opens it and she slips out*)

MENDEL (*Half-seen at the door, expostulating*): You, too, Miss Revendal—?

(*Re-enters*)

Oh, David, you have driven away all your friends.

DAVID (*Going to window and looking after* VERA): Not all, uncle. Not all.

(*He throws his arms boyishly round his uncle*)

I am so happy.

MENDEL: Happy?

DAVID: She loves me—Vera loves me.

MENDEL: Vera?

DAVID: Miss Revendal.

MENDEL: Have you lost your wits?

(*He throws* DAVID *off*)

DAVID: I don't wonder you're amazed. Maybe you think *I* wasn't. It is as if an angel should stoop down—

MENDEL (*Hoarsely*): This is true? This is not some stupid *Purim* joke?

DAVID: True and sacred as the sunrise.

MENDEL: But you are a Jew!

DAVID: Yes, and just think! She was bred up to despise Jews—her father was a Russian baron—

MENDEL: If she was the daughter of fifty barons, you cannot marry her.

DAVID (*In pained amaze*): Uncle!

(*Slowly*)

Then your hankering after the synagogue was serious after all.

MENDEL: It is not so much the synagogue—it is the call of our blood through immemorial generations.

DAVID: *You* say that! You who have come to the heart of the Crucible, where the roaring fires of God are fusing our race with all the others.

MENDEL (*Passionately*): Not *our* race, not your race and mine.

DAVID: What immunity has our race?

(*Meditatively*)

The pride and the prejudice, the dreams and the sacrifices, the traditions and the superstitions, the fasts and the feasts, things noble and things sordid—they must all into the Crucible.

MENDEL (*With prophetic fury*): The Jew has been tried in a thousand fires and only tempered and annealed.

DAVID: Fires of hate, not fires of love. That is what melts.

MENDEL (*Sneeringly*): So I see.

DAVID: Your sneer is false. The love that melted me was not Vera's—it was the love *America* showed me—the day she gathered me to her breast.

MENDEL (*Speaking passionately and rapidly*): Many countries have gathered us. Holland took us when we were driven from Spain—but we did not become Dutchmen. Turkey took us when Germany oppressed us, but we have not become Turks.

DAVID: These countries were not in the making. They were old civilizations stamped with the seal of creed. In such countries the Jew may be right to stand out. But here in this new secular Republic we must look forward—

MENDEL (*Passionately interrupting*): We must look backwards, too.

DAVID (*Hysterically*): To what? To Kishineff?

(*As if seeing his vision*)

To that butcher's face directing the slaughter? To those—?

MENDEL (*Alarmed*): Hush! Calm yourself!

DAVID (*Struggling with himself*): Yes, I will calm myself—but how else shall I calm myself save by forgetting all that nightmare of religions and races, save by holding out my hands with prayer and music toward the Republic of Man and the Kingdom of God! The Past I cannot mend—its evil outlines are stamped in immortal rigidity. Take away the hope that I can mend the Future, and you make me mad.

MENDEL: You are mad already—your dreams are mad—the Jew is hated here as everywhere—you are false to your race.

DAVID: I keep faith with America. I have faith America will keep faith with us.

(*He raises his hands in religious rapture toward the flag over the door*)

Flag of our great Republic, guardian of our homes, whose stars and—

MENDEL: Spare me that rigmarole. Go out and marry your Gentile and be happy.

DAVID: You turn me out?

MENDEL: Would you stay and break my mother's heart? You know she would mourn for you with the rending of garments and the seven days' sitting on the floor. Go! You have cast off the God of our fathers!

DAVID (*Thundrously*): And the God of our children—does *He* demand no service?

(*Quieter, coming toward his uncle and touching him affectionately on the shoulder*)

You are right—I do need a wider world.

(*Expands his lungs*)

I must go away.

MENDEL: Go, then—I'll hide the truth—she must never suspect—lest she mourn you as dead.

FRAU QUIXANO (*Outside, in the kitchen*): Ha! Ha! Ha! Ha! Ha!

(*Both men turn toward the kitchen and listen*)

KATHLEEN: Ha! Ha! Ha! Ha! Ha!

FRAU QUIXANO AND KATHLEEN: Ha! Ha! Ha! Ha! Ha!

MENDEL (*Bitterly*): A merry *Purim*!

(*The kitchen door opens and remains ajar. FRAU QUIXANO rushes in, carrying DAVID's violin and bow. KATHLEEN looks in, grinning*)

FRAU QUIXANO (*Hilariously*): *Nu spiel noch! spiel!*

(*She holds the violin and bow appealingly toward DAVID*)

MENDEL (*Putting out a protesting hand*): No, no, David—I couldn't bear it.

DAVID: But I must! You said she mustn't suspect.

(*He looks lovingly at her as he loudly utters these words, which are unintelligible to her*)

And it may be the last time I shall ever play for her.

(*Changing to a mock merry smile as he takes the violin and bow from her*)

*Gewiss*, Granny!

(*He starts the same old Slavic dance*)

FRAU QUIXANO (*Childishly pleased*): He! He! He!

(*She claps on a false grotesque nose from her pocket*)

DAVID (*Torn between laughter and tears*): Ha! Ha! Ha! Ha! Ha!

MENDEL (*Shocked*): *Mutter!*

FRAU QUIXANO: *Un' du auch!*

(*She claps another false nose on* MENDEL, *laughing in childish glee at the effect. Then she starts dancing to the music, and* KATHLEEN *slips in and joyously dances beside her*)

DAVID (*Joining tearfully in the laughter*): Ha! Ha! Ha! Ha! Ha!

(*The curtain falls quickly. It rises again upon the picture of* FRAU QUIXANO *fallen back into a chair, exhausted with laughter, fanning herself with her apron, while* KATHLEEN *has dropped breathless across the arm of the armchair;* DAVID *is still playing on, and* MENDEL, *his false nose torn off, stands by, glowering. The curtain falls again and rises upon a final tableau of* DAVID *in his cloak and hat, stealing out of the door with his violin, casting a sad farewell glance at the old woman and at the home which has sheltered him*)

# Act III

*April, about a month later. The scene changes to* Miss Revendal'*s sitting-room at the Settlement House on a sunny day. Simple, pretty furniture: a sofa, chairs, small table, etc. An open piano with music. Flowers and books about. Fine art reproductions on walls. The fireplace is on the left. A door on the left leads to the hall, and a door on the right to the interior. A servant enters from the left, ushering in* Baron *and* Baroness Revendal *and* Quincy Davenport. *The* Baron *is a tall, stern, grizzled man of military bearing, with a narrow, fanatical forehead and martinet manners, but otherwise of honest and distinguished appearance, with a short, well-trimmed white beard and well-cut European clothes. Although his dignity is diminished by the constant nervous suspiciousness of the Russian official, it is never lost; his nervousness, despite its comic side, being visibly the tragic shadow of his position. His English has only a touch of the foreign in accent and vocabulary and is much superior to his wife's, which comes to her through her French. The* Baroness *is pretty and dressed in red in the height of Paris fashion, but blazes with barbaric jewels at neck and throat and wrist. She gestures freely with her hand, which, when ungloved, glitters with heavy rings. She is much younger than the* Baron *and self-consciously fascinating. Her parasol, which matches her costume, suggests the sunshine without.* Quincy Davenport *is in a smart spring suit with a motor dust-coat and cap, which last he lays down on the mantelpiece.*

Servant: Miss Revendal is on the roof-garden. I'll go and tell her.
(*Exit, toward the hall*)
Baron: A marvellous people, you Americans. Gardens in the sky!
Quincy: Gardens, forsooth! We plant a tub and call it Paradise. No, Baron. New York is the great stone desert.
Baroness: But ze big beautiful Park vere ve drove tru?
Quincy: No taste, Baroness, modern sculpture and menageries! Think of the Medici gardens at Rome.
Baroness: Ah, Rome!
(*With an ecstatic sigh, she drops into an armchair. Then she takes out a dainty cigarette-case, pulls off her right-hand glove, exhibiting her rings, and chooses a cigarette. The* Baron, *seeing this, produces his match-box*)
Quincy: And now, dear Baron Revendal, having brought you safely to the den of the lioness—if I may venture to call your daughter so—I must leave *you* to do the taming, eh?

Baron: You are always of the most amiable.

(*He strikes a match*)

Baroness: *Tout à fait charmant.*

(*The* Baron *lights her cigarette*)

Quincy (*Bows gallantly*): Don't mention it. I'll just have my auto take me to the Club, and then I'll send it back for you.

Baroness: Ah, zank you—zat street-car looks horreeble.

(*She puffs out smoke*)

Baron: Quite impossible. What is to prevent an anarchist sitting next to you and shooting out your brains?

Quincy: We haven't much of that here—I don't mean brains. Ha! Ha! Ha!

Baron: But I saw desperadoes spying as we came off your yacht.

Quincy: Oh, that was newspaper chaps.

Baron (*Shakes his head*): No—they are circulating my appearance to all the gang in the States. They took snapshots.

Quincy: Then you're quite safe from recognition.

(*He sniggers*)

Didn't they ask you questions?

Baron: Yes, but I am a diplomat. I do not reply.

Quincy: That's not very diplomatic here. Ha! Ha!

Baron: *Diable!*

(*He claps his hand to his hip pocket, half-producing a pistol. The* Baroness *looks equally anxious*)

Quincy: What's up?

Baron (*Points to window, whispers hoarsely*): Regard! A hooligan peeped in!

Quincy (*Goes to window*): Only some poor devil come to the Settlement.

Baron (*Hoarsely*): But under his arm—a bomb!

Quincy (*Shaking his head smilingly*): A soup bowl.

Baroness: Ha! Ha! Ha!

Quincy: What makes you so nervous, Baron?

(*The* Baron *slips back his pistol, a little ashamed*)

Baroness: Ze Intellectuals and ze *Bund*, zey all hate my husband because he is faizful to Christ

(*Crossing herself*)

and ze Tsar.

Quincy: But the Intellectuals are in Russia.

BARON: They have their branches here—the refugees are the leaders—it is a diabolical network.

QUINCY: Well, anyhow, *we're* not in Russia, eh? No, no, Baron, you're quite safe. Still, you can keep my automobile as long as you like—I've plenty.

BARON: A thousand thanks.

(*Wiping his forehead*)

But surely no gentleman would sit in the public car, squeezed between working-men and shop-girls, not to say Jews and Blacks.

QUINCY: It *is* done here. But we shall change all that. Already we have a few taxi-cabs. Give us time, my dear Baron, give us time. You mustn't judge us by your European standard.

BARON: By the European standard, Mr. Davenport, you put our hospitality to the shame. From the moment you sent your yacht for us to Odessa—

QUINCY: Pray, don't ever speak of that again—you know how anxious I was to get you to New York.

BARON: Provided we have arrived in time!

QUINCY: That's all right, I keep telling you. They aren't married yet—

BARON (*Grinding his teeth and shaking his fist*): Those Jew-vermin—all my life I have suffered from them!

QUINCY: We all suffer from them.

BARONESS: Zey are ze pests of ze civilisation.

BARON: But this supreme insult Vera shall not put on the blood of the Revendals—not if I have to shoot her down with my own hand—and myself after!

QUINCY: No, no, Baron, that's not done here. Besides, if you shoot her down, where do *I* come in, eh?

BARON (*Puzzled*): Where *you* come in?

QUINCY: Oh, Baron! Surely you have guessed that it is not merely Jew-hate, but—er—Christian love. Eh?

(*Laughing uneasily*)

BARON: You!

BARONESS (*Clapping her hands*): Oh, *charmant, charmant*! But it ees a romance!

BARON: But you are married!

BARONESS (*Downcast*): *Ah, oui. Quel dommage*, vat a peety!

QUINCY: You forget, Baron, we are in America. The law giveth and the law taketh away.

(*He sniggers*)

BARONESS: It ees a vonderful country! But your vife—*hein?*—vould she consent?

QUINCY: She's mad to get back on the stage—I'll run a theatre for her. It's your daughter's consent that's the real trouble—she won't see me because I lost my temper and told her to stop with her Jew. So I look to you to straighten things out.

BARONESS: *Mais parfaitement.*

BARON (*Frowning at her*): You go too quick, Katusha. What influence have I on Vera? And *you* she has never even seen! To kick out the Jew-beast is one thing. . .

QUINCY: Well, anyhow, don't *shoot* her—shoot the beast rather.

(*Sniggeringly*)

BARON: Shooting is too good for the enemies of Christ.

(*Crossing himself*)

At Kishineff we stick the swine.

QUINCY (*Interested*): Ah! I read about that. Did you see the massacre?

BARON: Which one? Give me a cigarette, Katusha.

(*She obeys*)

We've had several Jew-massacres in Kishineff.

QUINCY: Have you? The papers only boomed one—four or five years ago—about Easter time, I think—

BARON: Ah, yes—when the Jews insulted the procession of the Host!

(*Taking a light from the cigarette in his wife's mouth*)

QUINCY: Did they? I thought—

BARON (*Sarcastically*): I daresay. That's the lies they spread in the West. They have the Press in their hands, damn 'em. But you see I was on the spot.

(*He drops into a chair*)

I had charge of the whole district.

QUINCY (*Startled*): You!

BARON: Yes, and I hurried a regiment up to teach the blaspheming brutes manners—

(*He puffs out a leisurely cloud*)

QUINCY (*Whistling*): Whew! . . . I—I say, old chap, I mean Baron, you'd better not say that here.

BARON: Why not? I am proud of it.

BARONESS: My husband vas decorated for it—he has ze order of St. Vladimir.

ISRAEL ZANGWILL

BARON (*Proudly*): Second class! Shall we allow these bigots to mock at all we hold sacred? The Jews are the deadliest enemies of our holy autocracy and of the only orthodox Church. Their *Bund* is behind all the Revolution.

BARONESS: A plague-spot muz be cut out!

QUINCY: Well, I'd keep it dark if I were you. Kishineff is a back number, and we don't take much stock in the new massacres. Still, we're a bit queamish—

BARON: Squeamish! Don't you lynch and roast your niggers?

QUINCY: Not officially. Whereas your Black Hundreds—

BARON: Black Hundreds! My dear Mr. Davenport, they are the white hosts of Christ

(*Crossing himself*)

and of the Tsar, who is God's vicegerent on earth. Have you not read the works of our sainted Pobiedonostzeff, Procurator of the Most Holy Synod?

QUINCY: Well, of course, I always felt there was another side to it, but still—

BARONESS: Perhaps he has right, Alexis. Our Ambassador vonce told me ze Americans are more sentimental zan civilised.

BARON: Ah, let them wait till they have ten million vermin overrunning *their* country—we shall see how long they will be sentimental. Think of it! A burrowing swarm creeping and crawling everywhere, ugh! They ruin our peasantry with their loans and their drink shops, ruin our army with their revolutionary propaganda, ruin our professional classes by snatching all the prizes and professorships, ruin our commercial classes by monopolising our sugar industries, our oil-fields, our timber-trade. . . Why, if we gave them equal rights, our Holy Russia would be entirely run by them.

BARONESS: *Mon dieu! C'est vrai.* Ve real Russians vould become slaves.

QUINCY: Then what are you going to do with them?

BARON: One-third will be baptized, one-third massacred, the other third emigrated here.

(*He strikes a match to relight his cigarette*)

QUINCY (*Shudderingly*): Thank you, my dear Baron,—you've already sent me one Jew too many. We're going to stop all alien immigration.

BARON: To stop *all* alien—? But that is barbarous!

QUINCY: Well, don't let us waste our time on the Jew-problem. . . our own little Jew-problem is enough, eh? Get rid of this little fiddler. Then *I* may have a look in. Adieu, Baron.

BARON: Adieu.

(*Holding his hand*)

But you are not really serious about Vera?

(*The* BARONESS *makes a gesture of annoyance*)

QUINCY: Not serious, Baron? Why, to marry her is the only thing I have ever wanted that I couldn't get. It is torture! Baroness, I rely on your sympathy.

(*He kisses her hand with a pretentious foreign air*)

BARONESS (*In sentimental approval*): *Ah! l'amour! l'amour!*

(*Exit* QUINCY DAVENPORT, *taking his cap in passing*)

You might have given him a little encouragement, Alexis.

BARON: Silence, Katusha. I only tolerated the man in Europe because he was a link with Vera.

BARONESS: You accepted his yacht and his—

BARON: If I had known his loose views on divorce—

BARONESS: I am sick of your scruples. You are ze only poor official in Bessarabia.

BARON: Be silent! Have I not forbidden—?

BARONESS (*Petulantly*): Forbidden! Forbidden! All your life you have served ze Tsar, and you cannot afford a single automobile. A millionaire son-in-law is just vat you owe me.

BARON: What I owe you?

BARONESS: Yes, ven I married you, I vas tinking you had a good position. I did not know you were too honest to use it. You vere not open viz me, Alexis.

BARON: You knew I was a Revendal. The Revendals keep their hands clean. . .

(*With a sudden start he tiptoes noiselessly to the door leading to the hall and throws it open. Nobody is visible. He closes it shamefacedly*)

BARONESS (*Has shared his nervousness till the door was opened, but now bursts into mocking laughter*): If you thought less about your precious safety, and more about me and Vera—

BARON: Hush! You do not know Vera. You saw I was even afraid to give my name. She might have sent me away as she sent away the Tsar's plate of mutton.

BARONESS: The Tsar's plate of—?

ISRAEL ZANGWILL

BARON: Did I never tell you? When she was only a school-girl—at the Imperial High School—the Tsar on his annual visit tasted the food, and Vera, as the show pupil, was given the honour of finishing his Majesty's plate.

BARONESS (*In incredulous horror*): And she sent it avay?

BARON: Gave it to a servant.

(*Awed silence*)

And then you think I can impose a husband on her. No, Katusha, I have to win her love for myself, not for millionaires.

BARONESS (*Angry again*): Alvays so affrightfully selfish!

BARON: I have no control over her, I tell you!

(*Bitterly*)

I never could control my womenkind.

BARONESS: Because you zink zey are your soldiers. Silence! Halt! Forbidden! Right Veel! March!

BARON (*Sullenly*): I wish I did think they were my soldiers—I might try the lash.

BARONESS (*Springing up angrily, shakes parasol at him*): You British barbarian!

VERA (*Outside the door leading to the interior*): Yes, thank you, Miss Andrews. I know I have visitors.

BARON (*Ecstatically*): Vera's voice!

(*The* BARONESS *lowers her parasol. He looks yearningly toward the door. It opens. Enter* VERA *with inquiring gaze*)

VERA (*With a great shock of surprise*): Father!!

BARON: *Verotschka!* My dearest darling! . . .

(*He makes a movement toward her, but is checked by her irresponsiveness*)

Why, you've grown more beautiful than ever.

VERA: You in New York!

BARON: The Baroness wished to see America. Katusha, this is my daughter.

BARONESS (*In sugared sweetness*): And mine, too, if she vill let me love her.

VERA (*Bowing coldly, but still addressing her father*): But how? When?

BARON: We have just come and—

BARONESS (*Dashing in*): Zat charming young man lent us his yacht— he is adoràhble.

VERA: What charming young man?

BARONESS: Ah, she has many, ze little coquette—ha! ha! ha!

(*She touches* VERA *playfully with her parasol*)

BARON: We wished to give you a pleasant surprise.

VERA: It is certainly a surprise.

BARON (*Chilled*): You are not very. . . daughterly.

VERA: Do you remember when you last saw me? You did not claim me as a daughter then.

BARON (*Covers his eyes with his hand*): Do not recall it; it hurts too much.

VERA: I was in the dock.

BARON: It was horrible. I hated you for the devil of rebellion that had entered into your soul. But I thanked God when you escaped.

VERA (*Softened*): I think I was more sorry for you than for myself. I hope, at least, no suspicion fell on you.

BARONESS (*Eagerly*): But it did—an avalanche of suspicion. He is still buried under it. Vy else did they make Skovaloff Ambassador instead of him? Even now he risks everyting to see you again. Ah, *mon enfant*, you owe your fazer a grand reparation!

VERA: What reparation can I possibly make?

BARON (*Passionately*): You can love me again, Vera.

BARONESS (*Stamping foot*): Alexis, you are interrupting—

VERA: I fear, father, we have grown too estranged—our ideas are so opposite—

BARON: But not now, Vera, surely not now? You are no longer

(*He lowers his voice and looks around*)

a Revolutionist?

VERA: Not with bombs, perhaps. I thank Heaven I was caught before I had done any *practical* work. But if you think I accept the order of things, you are mistaken. In Russia I fought against the autocracy—

BARON: Hush! Hush!

(*He looks round nervously*)

VERA: Here I fight against the poverty. No, father, a woman who has once heard the call will always be a wild creature.

BARON: But

(*Lowering his voice*)

those revolutionary Russian clubs here—you are not a member?

VERA: I do not believe in Revolutions carried on at a safe distance. I have found my life-work in America.

BARON: I am enchanted, Vera, enchanted.

Baroness (*Gushingly*): Permit me to kiss you, *belle enfant*.

Vera: I do not know you enough yet; I will kiss my father.

Baron (*With a great cry of joy*): Vera!

(*He embraces her passionately*)

At last! At last! I have found my little Vera again!

Vera: No, father, *your* Vera belongs to Russia with her mother and the happy days of childhood. But for their sakes—

(*She breaks down in emotion*)

Baron: Ah, your poor mother!

Baroness (*Tartly*): Alexis, I perceive I am too many!

(*She begins to go toward the door*)

Baron: No, no, Katusha. Vera will learn to love you, too.

Vera (*To* Baroness): What does my loving you matter? I can never return to Russia.

Baroness (*Pausing*): But ve can come here—often—ven you are married.

Vera (*Surprised*): When I am married?

(*Softly, blushing*)

You know?

Baroness (*Smiling*): Ve know zat charming young man adores ze floor your foot treads on!

Vera (*Blushing*): You have seen David?

Baron (*Hoarsely*): David!

(*He clenches his fist*)

Baroness (*Half aside, as much gestured as spoken*): Sh! Leave it to me.

(*Sweetly*)

Oh, no, ve have not seen David.

Vera (*Looking from one to the other*): Not seen—? Then what—whom are you talking about?

Baroness: About zat handsome, quite adoràhble Mr. Davenport.

Vera: Davenport!

Baroness: Who combines ze manners of Europe viz ze millions of America!

Vera (*Breaks into girlish laughter*): Ha! Ha! Ha! So Mr. Davenport has been talking to you! But you all seem to forget one small point— bigamy is not permitted even to millionaires.

Baroness: Ah, not boz at vonce, but—

Vera: And do you think I would take another woman's leavings? No, not even if she were dead.

BARONESS: You are insulting!

VERA: I beg your pardon—I wasn't even thinking of you. Father, to put an end at once to this absurd conversation, let me inform you I am already engaged.

BARON (*Trembling, hoarse*): By name, David.

VERA: Yes—David Quixano.

BARON: A Jew!

VERA: How did you know? Yes, he is a Jew, a noble Jew.

BARON: A Jew noble!

(*He laughs bitterly*)

VERA: Yes—even as you esteem nobility—by pedigree. In Spain his ancestors were hidalgos, favourites at the Court of Ferdinand and Isabella; but in the great expulsion of 1492 they preferred exile in Poland to baptism.

BARON: And you, a Revendal, would mate with an unbaptized dog?

VERA: Dog! You call my husband a dog!

BARON: Husband! God in heaven—are you married already?

VERA: No! But not being unemployed millionaires like Mr. Davenport, we hold even our troth eternal.

(*Calmer*)

Our poverty, not your prejudice, stands in the way of our marriage. But David is a musician of genius, and some day—

BARONESS: A fiddler in a beer-hall! She prefers a fiddler to a millionaire of ze first families of America!

VERA (*Contemptuously*): First families! I told you David's family came to Poland in 1492—some months before America was discovered.

BARON: Christ save us! You have become a Jewess!

VERA: No more than David has become a Christian. We were already at one—all honest people are. Surely, father, all religions must serve the same God—since there is only one God to serve.

BARONESS: But ze girl is an ateist!

BARON: Silence, Katusha! Leave me to deal with my daughter.

(*Changing tone to pathos, taking her face between his hands*)

Oh, Vera, *Verotschka*, my dearest darling, I had sooner you had remained buried in Siberia than that—

(*He breaks down*)

VERA (*Touched, sitting beside him*): For you, father, I *was* as though buried in Siberia. Why did you come here to stab yourself afresh?

BARON: I wish to God I had come here earlier. I wish I had not been so nervous of Russian spies. Ah, *Verotschka*, if you only knew how I have pored over the newspaper pictures of you, and the reports of your life in this Settlement!

VERA: You asked me not to send letters.

BARON: I know, I know—and yet sometimes I felt as if I could risk Siberia myself to read your dear, dainty handwriting again.

VERA (*Still more softened*): Father, if you love me so much, surely you will love David a little too—for my sake.

BARON (*Dazed*): I—love—a Jew? Impossible.

(*He shudders*)

VERA (*Moving away, icily*): Then so is any love from me to you. You have chosen to come back into my life, and after our years of pain and separation I would gladly remember only my old childish affection. But not if you hate David. You must make your choice.

BARON (*Pitifully*): Choice? I have no choice. Can I carry mountains? No more can I love a Jew.

(*He rises resolutely*)

BARONESS (*Who has turned away, fretting and fuming, turns back to her husband, clapping her hands*): Bravo!

VERA (*Going to him again, coaxingly*): I don't ask you to carry mountains, but to drop the mountains you carry—the mountains of prejudice. Wait till you see him.

BARON: I will not see him.

VERA: Then you will hear him—he is going to make music for all the world. You can't escape him, *papasha*, you with your love of music, any more than you escaped Rubinstein.

BARONESS: Rubinstein vas not a Jew.

VERA: Rubinstein was a Jewish boy-genius, just like my David.

BARONESS: But his parents vere baptized soon after his birth. I had it from his patroness, ze Grande Duchesse Helena Pavlovna.

VERA: And did the water outside change the blood within? Rubinstein was our Court pianist and was decorated by the Tsar. And you, the Tsar's servant, dare to say you could not meet a Rubinstein.

BARON (*Wavering*): I did not say I could not meet a *Rubinstein*.

VERA: You practically said so. David will be even greater than Rubinstein. Come, father, I'll telephone for him; he is only round the corner.

BARONESS (*Excitedly*): Ve vill not see him!

VERA (*Ignoring her*): He shall bring his violin and play to you. There! You see, little father, you are already less frowning—now take that last wrinkle out of your forehead.

(*She caresses his forehead*)

Never mind! David will smooth it out with his music as his Biblical ancestor smoothed that surly old Saul.

BARONESS: Ve vill not hear him!

BARON: Silence, Katusha! Oh, my little Vera, I little thought when I let you study music at Petersburg—

VERA (*Smiling wheedlingly*): That I should marry a musician. But you see, little father, it all ends in music after all. Now I will go and perform on the telephone, I'm not angel enough to bear one in here.

(*She goes toward the door of the hall, smiling happily*)

BARON (*With a last agonized cry of resistance*): Halt!

VERA (*Turning, makes mock military salute*): Yes, *papasha*.

BARON (*Overcome by her roguish smile*): You—I—he—do you love this J—this David so much?

VERA (*Suddenly tragic*): It would kill me to give him up.

(*Resuming smile*)

But don't let us talk of funerals on this happy day of sunshine and reunion.

(*She kisses her hand to him and exit toward the hall*)

BARONESS (*Angrily*): You are in her hands as vax!

BARON: She is the only child I have ever had, Katusha. Her baby arms curled round my neck; in her baby sorrows her wet face nestled against little father's.

(*He drops on a chair, and leans his head on the table*)

BARONESS (*Approaching tauntingly*): So you vill have a Jew son-in-law!

BARON: You don't know what it meant to me to feel her arms round me again.

BARONESS: And a hook-nosed brat to call you grandpapa, and nestle his greasy face against yours.

BARON (*Banging his fist on the table*): Don't drive me mad!

(*His head drops again*)

BARONESS: Then drive me home—I vill not meet him. . . Alexis!

(*She taps him on the shoulder with her parasol. He does not move*)

Alexis Ivanovitch! Do you not listen! . . .

(*She stamps her foot*)

Zen I go to ze hotel alone.

*(She walks angrily toward the hall. Just before she reaches the door, it opens, and the servant ushers in* HERR PAPPELMEISTER *with his umbrella. The* BARONESS's *tone changes instantly to a sugared society accent)*

How do you do, Herr Pappelmeister?

*(She extends her hand, which he takes limply)*

You don't remember me? *Non?*

*(Exit servant)*

Ve vere with Mr. Quincy Davenport at Wiesbaden—ze Baroness Revendal.

PAPPELMEISTER: *So!*

*(He drops her hand)*

BARONESS: Yes, it vas ze Baron's entousiasm for you zat got you your present position.

PAPPELMEISTER *(Arching his eyebrows)*: *So!*

BARONESS: Yes—zere he is!

*(She turns toward the* BARON*)*

Alexis, rouse yourself!

*(She taps him with her parasol)*

Zis American air makes ze Baron so sleepy.

BARON *(Rises dazedly and bows)*: Charmed to meet you, Herr—

BARONESS: Pappelmeister! You remember ze great Pappelmeister.

BARON *(Waking up, becomes keen)*: Ah, yes, yes, charmed—why do you never bring your orchestra to Russia, Herr Pappelmeister?

PAPPELMEISTER *(Surprised)*: Russia? It never occurred to me to go to Russia—she seems so uncivilised.

BARONESS *(Angry)*: Uncivilised! Vy, ve have ze finest restaurants in ze vorld! And ze best telephones!

PAPPELMEISTER: *So?*

BARONESS: Yes, and the most beautiful ballets—Russia is affrightfully misunderstood.

*(She sweeps away in burning indignation.* PAPPELMEISTER *murmurs in deprecation. Re-enter* VERA *from the hall. She is gay and happy)*

VERA: He is coming round at once—

*(She utters a cry of pleased surprise)*

Herr Pappelmeister! This is indeed a pleasure!

*(She gives* PAPPELMEISTER *her hand, which he kisses)*

BARONESS *(Sotto voce to the* BARON*)*: Let us go before he comes.

*(The* BARON *ignores her, his eyes hungrily on* VERA*)*

PAPPELMEISTER *(To* VERA*)*: But I come again—you have visitors.

VERA (*Smiling*): Only my father and—

PAPPELMEISTER (*Surprised*): Your fader? *Ach so!*

(*He taps his forehead*)

Revendal!

BARONESS (*Sotto voce to the* BARON): I vill not meet a Jew, I tell you.

PAPPELMEISTER: But you vill vant to talk to your fader, and all *I* vant is Mr. Quixano's address. De Irish maiden at de house says de bird is flown.

VERA (*Gravely*): I don't know if I ought to tell you where the new nest is—

PAPPELMEISTER (*Disappointed*): *Ach!*

VERA (*Smiling*): But I will produce the bird.

PAPPELMEISTER (*Looks round*): You vill broduce Mr. Quixano?

VERA (*Merrily*): By clapping my hands.

(*Mysteriously*)

I am a magician.

BARON (*Whose eyes have been glued on* VERA): You are, indeed! I don't know how you have bewitched me.

(*The* BARONESS *glares at him*)

VERA: Dear little father!

(*She crosses to him and strokes his hair*)

Herr Pappelmeister, tell father about Mr. Quixano's music.

PAPPELMEISTER (*Shaking his head*): Music cannot be talked about.

VERA (*Smiling*): That's a nasty one for the critics. But tell father what a genius Da—Mr. Quixano is.

BARONESS (*Desperately intervening*): Good-bye, Vera.

(*She thrusts out her hand, which* VERA *takes*)

I have a headache. You muz excuse me. Herr Pappelmeister, *au plaisir de vous revoir.*

(PAPPELMEISTER *hastens to the door, which he holds open. The* BARONESS *turns and glares at the* BARON)

BARON (*Agitated*): Let me see you to the auto—

BARONESS: You could see me to ze hotel almost as quick.

BARON (*To* VERA): I won't say good-bye, *Verotschka*—I shall be back.

(*He goes toward the hall, then turns*)

You will keep your Rubinstein waiting?

(VERA *smiles lovingly*)

BARONESS: You are keeping *me* vaiting.

(*He turns quickly. Exeunt* BARON *and* BARONESS)

PAPPELMEISTER: And now broduce Mr. Quixano!

VERA: Not so fast. What are you going to do with him?

PAPPELMEISTER: Put him in my orchestra!

VERA (*Ecstatic*): Oh, you dear!

(*Then her tone changes to disappointment*)

But he won't go into Mr. Davenport's orchestra.

PAPPELMEISTER: It is no more Mr. Davenport's orchestra. He fired me, don't you remember? Now I boss—how say you in American?

VERA (*Smiling*): Your own show.

PAPPELMEISTER: *Ja*, my own band. Ven I left dat comic opera millionaire, dey all shtick to me almost to von man.

VERA: How nice of them!

PAPPELMEISTER: All egsept de Christian—he vas de von man. He shtick to de millionaire. So I lose my brincipal first violin.

VERA: And Mr. Quixano is to—oh, how delightful!

(*She claps her hands girlishly*)

PAPPELMEISTER (*Looks round mischievously*): *Ach*, de magic failed.

VERA (*Puzzled*): Eh!

PAPPELMEISTER: You do not broduce him. You clap de hands—but you do not broduce him. Ha! Ha! Ha!

(*He breaks into a great roar of genial laughter*)

VERA (*Chiming in merrily*): Ha! Ha! Ha! But I said I have to know everything first. Will he get a good salary?

PAPPELMEISTER: Enough to keep a vife and eight children!

VERA (*Blushing*): But he hasn't a—

PAPPELMEISTER: No, but de Christian had—he get de same—I mean salary, ha! ha! ha! not children. Den he can be independent— vedder de fool-public like his American symphony or not—*nicht wahr?*

VERA: You *are* good to us—

(*Hastily correcting herself*)

to Mr. Quixano.

PAPPELMEISTER (*Smiling*): And aldough you cannot broduce him, I broduce his symphony. *Was?*

VERA: Oh, Herr Pappelmeister! You are an angel.

PAPPELMEISTER: *Nein, nein, mein liebes Kind!* I fear I haf not de correct shape for an angel.

(*He laughs heartily. A knock at the door from the hall*)

VERA (*Merrily*): *Now* I clap my hands.

*(She claps)*

Come!

*(The door opens)*

Behold him!

*(She makes a conjurer's gesture. DAVID, bare-headed, carrying his fiddle, opens the door, and stands staring in amazement at PAPPELMEISTER)*

DAVID: I thought you asked me to meet your father.

PAPPELMEISTER: She is a magician. She has changed us.

*(He waves his umbrella)*

Hey presto, *was?* Ha! Ha! Ha!

*(He goes to DAVID, and shakes hands)*

*Und wie geht's?* I hear you've left home.

DAVID: Yes, but I've such a bully cabin—

PAPPELMEISTER *(Alarmed)*: You are sailing avay?

VERA *(Laughing)*: No, no—that's only his way of describing his two-dollar-a-month garret.

DAVID: Yes—my state-room on the top deck!

VERA *(Smiling)*: Six foot square.

DAVID: But three other passengers aren't squeezed in, and it never pitches and tosses. It's heavenly.

PAPPELMEISTER *(Smiling)*: And from heaven you flew down to blay in dat beer-hall. *Was?*

*(DAVID looks surprised)*

*I* heard you.

DAVID: You! What on earth did you go *there* for?

PAPPELMEISTER: Vat on earth does one go to a beer-hall for? Ha! Ha! Ha! For vawter! Ha! Ha! Ha! Ven I hear you blay, I dink mit myself—if my blans succeed and I get Carnegie Hall for Saturday Symphony Concerts, dat boy shall be one of my first violins. *Was?*

*(He slaps DAVID on the left shoulder)*

DAVID *(Overwhelmed, ecstatic, yet wincing a little at the slap on his wound)*: Be one of your first—

*(Remembering)*

Oh, but it is impossible.

VERA *(Alarmed)*: Mr. Quixano! You must not refuse.

DAVID: But does Herr Pappelmeister know about the wound in my shoulder?

PAPPELMEISTER *(Agitated)*: You haf been vounded?

DAVID: Only a legacy from Russia—but it twinges in some weathers.

PAPPELMEISTER: And de pain ubsets your blaying?

DAVID: Not so much the pain—it's all the dreadful memories—

VERA (*Alarmed*): Don't talk of them.

DAVID: I *must* explain to Herr Pappelmeister—it wouldn't be fair.
Even now
(*Shuddering*)
there comes up before me the bleeding body of my mother, the cold,
fiendish face of the Russian officer, supervising the slaughter—

VERA: Hush! Hush!

DAVID (*Hysterically*): Oh, that butcher's face—there it is—hovering in
the air, that narrow, fanatical forehead, that—

PAPPELMEISTER (*Brings down his umbrella with a bang*): *Schluss!* No
man ever dared break down under me. My baton will beat avay all
dese faces and fancies. Out with your violin!
(*He taps his umbrella imperiously on the table*)
*Keinen Mut verlieren!*
(DAVID *takes out his violin from its case and puts it to his shoulder,*
PAPPELMEISTER *keeping up a hypnotic torrent of encouraging German cries*)
*Also! Fertig! Anfangen!*
(*He raises and waves his umbrella like a baton*)
Von, dwo, dree, four—

DAVID (*With a great sigh of relief*): Thanks, thanks—they are gone already.

PAPPELMEISTER: Ha! Ha! Ha! You see. And ven ve blay your
American symphony—

DAVID (*Dazed*): You will play my American symphony?

VERA (*Disappointed*): Don't you jump for joy?

DAVID (*Still dazed but ecstatic*): Herr Pappelmeister!
(*Changing back to despondency*)
But what certainty is there your Carnegie Hall audience would
understand me? It would be the same smart set.
(*He drops dejectedly into a chair and lays down his violin*)

PAPPELMEISTER: *Ach, nein.* Of course, some—ve can't keep peoble out
merely because dey pay for deir seats. *Was?*
(*He laughs*)

DAVID: It was always my dream to play it first to the new
immigrants—those who have known the pain of the old world and
the hope of the new.

PAPPELMEISTER: Try it on the dog. *Was?*

DAVID: Yes—on the dog that here will become a man!

PAPPELMEISTER (*Shakes his head*): I fear neider dogs nor men are a musical breed.

DAVID: The immigrants will not understand my music with their brains or their ears, but with their hearts and their souls.

VERA: Well, then, why shouldn't it be done here—on our Roof-Garden?

DAVID (*Jumping up*): A *Bas-Kôl*! A *Bas-Kôl*!

VERA: What *are* you talking?

DAVID: Hebrew! It means a voice from heaven.

VERA: Ah, but will Herr Pappelmeister consent?

PAPPELMEISTER (*Bowing*): Who can disobey a voice from heaven? . . . But ven?

VERA: On some holiday evening. . . Why not the Fourth of July?

DAVID (*Still more ecstatic*): Another *Bas-Kôl*! . . . . My American Symphony! Played to the People! Under God's sky! On Independence Day! With all the—

(*Waving his hand expressively, sighs voluptuously*)

That will be too perfect.

PAPPELMEISTER (*Smiling*): Dat has to be seen. You must permit me to invite—

DAVID (*In horror*): Not the musical critics!

PAPPELMEISTER (*Raising both hands with umbrella in equal horror*): *Gott bewahre!* But I'd like to invite all de persons in New York who really undershtand music.

VERA: Splendid! But should we have room?

PAPPELMEISTER: Room? I vant four blaces.

VERA (*Smiling*): You are severe! Mr. Davenport was right.

PAPPELMEISTER (*Smiling*): Perhaps de oders vill be out of town. *Also!*

(*Holding out his hand to* DAVID)

You come to Carnegie to-morrow at eleven. Yes? *Fräulein.*

(*Kisses her hand*)

*Auf Wiedersehen!*

(*Going*)

On de Roof-Garden—*nicht wahr?*

VERA (*Smiling*): Wind and weather permitting.

PAPPELMEISTER: I haf alvays mein umbrella. *Was?* Ha! Ha! Ha!

VERA (*Murmuring*): Isn't he a darling? Isn't he—?

PAPPELMEISTER (*Pausing suddenly*): But ve never settled de salary.

DAVID: Salary!

(*He looks dazedly from one to the other*)

For the honour of playing in your orchestra!

PAPPELMEISTER: Shylock!! . . . Never mind—ve settle de pound of flesh to-morrow. *Lebe wohl!*

(*Exit, the door closes*)

VERA (*Suddenly miserable*): How selfish of you, David!

DAVID: Selfish, Vera?

VERA: Yes—not to think of your salary. It looks as if you didn't really love me.

DAVID: Not love you? I don't understand.

VERA (*Half in tears*): Just when I was so happy to think that now we shall be able to marry.

DAVID: Shall we? Marry? On my salary as first violin?

VERA: Not if you don't want to.

DAVID: Sweetheart! Can it be true? How do you know?

VERA (*Smiling*): *I'm* not a Jew. I asked.

DAVID: My guardian angel!

(*Embracing her. He sits down, she lovingly at his feet*)

VERA (*Looking up at him*): Then you *do* care?

DAVID: What a question!

VERA: And you don't think wholly of your music and forget me?

DAVID: Why, you are behind all I write and play!

VERA (*With jealous passion*): Behind? But I want to be before! I want you to love me first, before everything.

DAVID: I do put you before everything.

VERA: You are sure? And nothing shall part us?

DAVID: Not all the seven seas could part you and me.

VERA: And you won't grow tired of me—not even when you are world-famous—?

DAVID (*A shade petulant*): Sweetheart, considering I should owe it all to you—

VERA (*Drawing his head down to her breast*): Oh, David! David! Don't be angry with poor little Vera if she doubts, if she wants to feel quite sure. You see father has talked so terribly, and after all I was brought up in the Greek Church, and we oughtn't to cause all this suffering unless—

DAVID: Those who love us *must* suffer, and *we* must suffer in their suffering. It is live things, not dead metals, that are being melted in the Crucible.

VERA: Still, we ought to soften the suffering as much as—

DAVID: Yes, but only Time can heal it.

VERA (*With transition to happiness*): But father seems half-reconciled already! Dear little father, if only he were not so narrow about Holy Russia!

DAVID: If only *my* folks were not so narrow about Holy Judea! But the ideals of the fathers shall not be foisted on the children. Each generation must live and die for its own dream.

VERA: Yes, David, yes. You are the prophet of the living present. I am so happy.

(*She looks up wistfully*)

You are happy, too?

DAVID: I am dazed—I cannot realise that all our troubles have melted away—it is so sudden.

VERA: You, David? Who always see everything in such rosy colours? Now that the whole horizon is one great splendid rose, you almost seem as if gazing out toward a blackness—

DAVID: We Jews are cheerful in gloom, mistrustful in joy. It is our tragic history—

VERA: But you have come to end the tragic history; to throw off the coils of the centuries.

DAVID (*Smiling again*): Yes, yes, Vera. You bring back my sunnier self. I must be a pioneer on the lost road of happiness. To-day shall be all joy, all lyric ecstasy.

(*He takes up his violin*)

Yes, I will make my old fiddle-strings *burst* with joy!

(*He dashes into a jubilant tarantella. After a few bars there is a knock at the door leading from the hall; their happy faces betray no sign of hearing it; then the door slightly opens, and* BARON REVENDAL's *head looks hesitatingly in. As* DAVID *perceives it, his features work convulsively, his string breaks with a tragic snap, and he totters backward into* VERA's *arms. Hoarsely*)

The face! The face!

VERA: David—my dearest!

DAVID (*His eyes closed, his violin clasped mechanically*): Don't be anxious—I shall be better soon—I oughtn't to have talked about it—the hallucination has never been so complete.

VERA: Don't speak—rest against Vera's heart—till it has passed away.

(*The* BARON *comes dazedly forward, half with a shocked sense of* VERA's *impropriety, half to relieve her of her burden. She motions him back*)

This is the work of your Holy Russia.

BARON (*Harshly*): What is the matter with him?

(DAVID's *violin and bow drop from his grasp and fall on the table*)

DAVID: The voice!

(*He opens his eyes, stares frenziedly at the* BARON, *then struggles out of* VERA's *arms*)

VERA (*Trying to stop him*): Dearest—

DAVID: Let me go.

(*He moves like a sleep-walker toward the paralysed* BARON, *puts out his hand, and testingly touches the face*)

BARON (*Shuddering back*): Hands off!

DAVID (*With a great cry*): A-a-a-h! It is flesh and blood. No, it is stone—the man of stone! Monster!

(*He raises his hand frenziedly*)

BARON (*Whipping out his pistol*): Back, dog!

(VERA *darts between them with a shriek*)

DAVID (*Frozen again, surveying the pistol stonily*): Ha! You want *my* life, too. Is the cry not yet loud enough?

BARON: The cry?

DAVID (*Mystically*): Can you not hear it? The voice of the blood of my brothers crying out against you from the ground? Oh, how can you bear not to turn that pistol against yourself and execute upon yourself the justice which Russia denies you?

BARON: Tush!

(*Pocketing the pistol a little shamefacedly*)

VERA: Justice on himself? For what?

DAVID: For crimes beyond human penalty, for obscenities beyond human utterance, for—

VERA: You are raving.

DAVID: Would to heaven I were!

VERA: But this is my father.

DAVID: Your father! . . . God!

(*He staggers*)

BARON (*Drawing her to him*): Come, Vera, I told you—

VERA (*Frantically, shrinking back*): Don't touch me!

BARON (*Starting back in amaze*): Vera!

VERA (*Hoarsely*): Say it's not true.

BARON: What is not true?

VERA: What David said. It was the mob that massacred—*you* had no hand in it.

BARON (*Sullenly*): I was there with my soldiers.

DAVID (*Leaning, pale, against a chair, hisses*): And you looked on with that cold face of hate—while my mother—my sister—

BARON (*Sullenly*): I could not see everything.

DAVID: Now and again you ordered your soldiers to fire—

VERA (*In joyous relief*): Ah, he *did* check the mob—he *did* tell his soldiers to fire.

DAVID: At any Jew who tried to defend himself.

VERA: Great God!

(*She falls on the sofa and buries her head on the cushion, moaning*)

Is there no pity in heaven?

DAVID: There was no pity on earth.

BARON: It was the People avenging itself, Vera. The People rose like a flood. It had centuries of spoliation to wipe out. The voice of the People is the voice of God.

VERA (*Moaning*): But you could have stopped them.

BARON: I had no orders to defend the foes of Christ and

(*Crossing himself*)

the Tsar. The People—

VERA: But you could have stopped them.

BARON: Who can stop a flood? I did my duty. A soldier's duty is not so pretty as a musician's.

VERA: But you could have stopped them.

BARON (*Losing all patience*): Silence! You talk like an ignorant girl, blinded by passion. The *pogrom* is a holy crusade. Are we Russians the first people to crush down the Jew? No—from the dawn of history the nations have had to stamp upon him—the Egyptians, the Assyrians, the Persians, the Babylonians, the Greeks, the Romans—

DAVID: Yes, it is true. Even Christianity did not invent hatred. But not till Holy Church arose were we burnt at the stake, and not till Holy Russia arose were our babes torn limb from limb. Oh, it is too much! Delivered from Egypt four thousand years ago, to be slaves to the Russian Pharaoh to-day.

(*He falls as if kneeling on a chair, and, leans his head on the rail*)

O God, shall we always be broken on the wheel of history? How long, O Lord, how long?

BARON (*Savagely*): Till you are all stamped out, ground into your dirt.

(*Tenderly*)

Look up, little Vera! You saw how *papasha* loves you—how he was ready to hold out his hand—and how this cur tried to bite it. Be calm—tell him a daughter of Russia cannot mate with dirt.

VERA: Father, I will be calm. I will speak without passion or blindness. I will tell David the truth. I was never absolutely sure of my love for him—perhaps that was why I doubted his love for me—often after our enchanted moments there would come a nameless uneasiness, some vague instinct, relic of the long centuries of Jew-loathing, some strange shrinking from his Christless creed—

BARON (*With an exultant cry*): Ah! She is a Revendal.

VERA: But now—

(*She rises and walks firmly toward* DAVID)

now, David, I come to you, and I say in the words of Ruth, thy people shall be my people and thy God my God!

(*She stretches out her hands to* DAVID)

BARON: You shameless—!

(*He stops as he perceives* DAVID *remains impassive*)

VERA (*With agonised cry*): David!

DAVID (*In low, icy tones*): You cannot come to me. There is a river of blood between us.

VERA: Were it seven seas, our love must cross them.

DAVID: Easy words to you. You never saw that red flood bearing the mangled breasts of women and the spattered brains of babes and sucklings. Oh!

(*He covers his eyes with his hands. The* BARON *turns away in gloomy impotence. At last* DAVID *begins to speak quietly, almost dreamily*)

It was your Easter, and the air was full of holy bells and the streets of holy processions—priests in black and girls in white and waving palms and crucifixes, and everybody exchanging Easter eggs and kissing one another three times on the mouth in token of peace and goodwill, and even the Jew-boy felt the spirit of love brooding over the earth, though he did not then know that this Christ, whom holy chants proclaimed re-risen, was born in the form of a brother Jew. And what added to the peace and holy joy was that our own Passover was shining before us. My mother had already made the raisin wine, and my greedy little brother Solomon had sipped it on the sly that very morning. We were all at home—all except my father—he was away in the little Synagogue at which he was cantor. Ah, such a voice he had—a voice of tears and thunder—when he prayed it was like a wounded soul beating at the gates of Heaven—but he sang even more beautifully in the ritual of home, and how we were looking forward to his hymns at the Passover table—

(*He breaks down. The* Baron *has gradually turned round under the spell of* David's *story and now listens hypnotised*)

I was playing my cracked little fiddle. Little Miriam was making her doll dance to it. Ah, that decrepit old china doll—the only one the poor child had ever had—I can see it now—one eye, no nose, half an arm. We were all laughing to see it caper to my music. . . My father flies in through the door, desperately clasping to his breast the Holy Scroll. We cry out to him to explain, and then we see that in that beloved mouth of song there is no longer a tongue—only blood. He tries to bar the door—a mob breaks in—we dash out through the back into the street. There are the soldiers—and the Face—

(Vera's *eyes involuntarily seek the face of her father, who shrinks away as their eyes meet*)

Vera (*In a low sob*): O God!

David: When I came to myself, with a curious aching in my left shoulder, I saw lying beside me a strange shapeless Something. . .

(David *points weirdly to the floor, and* Vera, *hunched forwards, gazes stonily at it, as if seeing the horror*)

By the crimson doll in what seemed a hand I knew it must be little Miriam. The doll was a dream of beauty and perfection beside the mutilated mass which was all that remained of my sister, of my mother, of greedy little Solomon— Oh! You Christians can only see that rosy splendour on the horizon of happiness. And the Jew didn't see rosily enough for you, ha! ha! ha! the Jew who gropes in one great crimson mist.

(*He breaks down in spasmodic, ironic, long-drawn, terrible laughter*)

Vera (*Trying vainly to tranquillise him*): Hush, David! Your laughter hurts more than tears. Let Vera comfort you.

(*She kneels by his chair, tries to put her arms round him*)

David (*Shuddering*): Take them away! Don't you feel the cold dead pushing between us?

Vera (*Unfaltering, moving his face toward her lips*): Kiss me!

David: I should feel the blood on my lips.

Vera: My love shall wipe it out.

DAVID: Love! Christian love!

(*He unwinds her clinging arms; she sinks prostrate on the floor as he rises*)

For this I gave up my people—darkened the home that sheltered me—there was always a still, small voice at my heart calling me back, but I heeded nothing—only the voice of the butcher's daughter.

(*Brokenly*)

Let me go home, let me go home.

(*He looks lingeringly at* VERA'S *prostrate form, but overcoming the instinct to touch and comfort her, begins tottering with uncertain pauses toward the door leading to the hall*)

BARON (*Extending his arms in relief and longing*): And here is *your* home, Vera!

(*He raises her gradually from the floor; she is dazed, but suddenly she becomes conscious of whose arms she is in, and utters a cry of repulsion*)

VERA: Those arms reeking from that crimson river!

(*She falls back*)

BARON (*Sullenly*): Don't echo that babble. You came to these arms often enough when they were fresh from the battlefield.

VERA: But not from the shambles! You heard what he called you. Not soldier—butcher! Oh, I dared to dream of happiness after my nightmare of Siberia, but you—you—

(*She breaks down for the first time in hysterical sobs*)

BARON (*Brokenly*): Vera! Little Vera! Don't cry! You stab me!

VERA: You thought you were ordering your soldiers to fire at the Jews, but it was my heart they pierced.

(*She sobs on*)

BARON: . . . And my own. . . But we will comfort each other. I will go to the Tsar myself—with my forehead to the earth—to beg for your pardon! . . . Come, put your wet face to little father's. . .

VERA (*Violently pushing his face away*): I hate you! I curse the day I was born your daughter!

(*She staggers toward the door leading to the interior. At the same moment* DAVID, *who has reached the door leading to the hall, now feeling subconsciously that* VERA *is going and that his last reason for lingering on is removed, turns the door-handle. The click attracts the* BARON'S *attention, he veers round*)

BARON (*To* DAVID): Halt!

(DAVID *turns mechanically.* VERA *drifts out through her door, leaving the two men face to face. The* BARON *beckons to* DAVID, *who as if hypnotised moves nearer. The* BARON *whips out his pistol, slowly crosses to* DAVID, *who stands as if awaiting his fate. The* BARON *hands the pistol to* DAVID)

You were right!

(*He steps back swiftly with a touch of stern heroism into the attitude of the culprit at a military execution, awaiting the bullet*)

Shoot me!

DAVID (*Takes the pistol mechanically, looks long and pensively at it as with a sense of its irrelevance. Gradually his arm droops and lets the pistol fall on the table, and there his hand touches a string of his violin, which yields a little note. Thus reminded of it, he picks up the violin, and as his fingers draw out the broken string he murmurs*): I must get a new string.

(*He resumes his dragging march toward the door, repeating maunderingly*)

I must get a new string.

(*The curtain falls*)

ISRAEL ZANGWILL

# Act IV

*Saturday, July 4, evening. The Roof-Garden of the Settlement House, showing a beautiful, far-stretching panorama of New York, with its irregular sky-buildings on the left, and the harbour with its Statue of Liberty on the right. Everything is wet and gleaming after rain. Parapet at the back. Elevator on the right. Entrance from the stairs on the left. In the sky hang heavy clouds through which thin, golden lines of sunset are just beginning to labour. DAVID is discovered on a bench, hugging his violin-case to his breast, gazing moodily at the sky. A muffled sound of applause comes up from below and continues with varying intensity through the early part of the scene. Through it comes the noise of the elevator ascending. MENDEL steps out and hurries forward.*

MENDEL: Come down, David! Don't you hear them shouting for you? (*He passes his hand over the wet bench*)

    Good heavens! You will get rheumatic fever!

DAVID: Why have you followed me?

MENDEL: Get up—everything is still damp.

DAVID (*Rising, gloomily*): Yes, there's a damper over everything.

MENDEL: Nonsense—the rain hasn't damped your triumph in the least. In fact, the more delicate effects wouldn't have gone so well in the open air. Listen!

DAVID: Let them shout. Who told you I was up here?

MENDEL: Miss Revendal, of course.

DAVID (*Agitated*): Miss Revendal? How should *she* know?

MENDEL (*Sullenly*): She seems to understand your crazy ways.

DAVID (*Passing his hand over his eyes*): Ah, *you* never understood me, uncle. . . How did she look? Was she pale?

MENDEL: Never mind about Miss Revendal. Pappelmeister wants you—the people insist on seeing you. Nobody can quiet them.

DAVID: They saw me all through the symphony in my place in the orchestra.

MENDEL: They didn't know you were the composer as well as the first violin. Now Miss Revendal has told them.

(*Louder applause*)

    There! Eleven minutes it has gone on—like for an office-seeker. You *must* come and show yourself.

DAVID: I won't—I'm not an office-seeker. Leave me to my misery.

MENDEL: Your misery? With all this glory and greatness opening before you? Wait till you're *my* age—

(*Shouts of* "QUIXANO!")

You hear! What is to be done with them?

DAVID: Send somebody on the platform to remind them this is the interval for refreshments!

MENDEL: Don't be cynical. You know your dearest wish was to melt these simple souls with your music. And now—

DAVID: Now I have only made my own stony.

MENDEL: You are right. You are stone all over—ever since you came back home to us. Turned into a pillar of salt, mother says—like Lot's wife.

DAVID: That was the punishment for looking backward. Ah, uncle, there's more sense in that old Bible than the Rabbis suspect. Perhaps that is the secret of our people's paralysis—we are always looking backward.

(*He drops hopelessly into an iron garden-chair behind him*)

MENDEL (*Stopping him before he touches the seat*): Take care—it's sopping wet. You don't look backward enough.

(*He takes out his handkerchief and begins drying the chair*)

DAVID (*Faintly smiling*): I thought you wanted the salt to melt.

MENDEL: It *is* melting a little if you can smile. Do you know, David, I haven't seen you smile since that *Purim* afternoon?

DAVID: You haven't worn a false nose since, uncle.

(*He laughs bitterly*)

Ha! Ha! Ha! Fancy masquerading in America because twenty-five centuries ago the Jews escaped a *pogrom* in Persia. Two thousand five hundred years ago! Aren't we uncanny?

(*He drops into the wiped chair*)

MENDEL (*Angrily*): Better you should leave us altogether than mock at us. I thought it was your Jewish heart that drove you back home to us; but if you are still hankering after Miss Revendal—

DAVID (*Pained*): Uncle!

MENDEL: I'd rather see you marry her than go about like this. You couldn't make the house any gloomier.

DAVID: Go back to the concert, please. They have quieted down.

MENDEL (*Hesitating*): And you?

DAVID: Oh, I'm not playing in the popular after-pieces. Pappelmeister guessed I'd be broken up with the stress of my own symphony—he has violins enough.

MENDEL: Then you don't want to carry this about.

(*Taking the violin from* DAVID'S *arms*)

DAVID (*Clinging to it*): Don't rob me of my music—it's all I have.

MENDEL: You'll spoil it in the wet. I'll take it home.

DAVID: No—

(*He suddenly catches sight of two figures entering from the left*—FRAU QUIXANO *and* KATHLEEN *clad in their best, and wearing tiny American flags in honour of Independence Day.* KATHLEEN *escorts the old lady, with the air of a guardian angel, on her slow, tottering course toward* DAVID. FRAU QUIXANO *is puffing and panting after the many stairs.* DAVID *jumps up in surprise, releases the violin-case to* MENDEL)

They at my symphony!

MENDEL: Mother *would* come—even though, being *Shabbos*, she had to walk.

DAVID: But wasn't she shocked at my playing on the Sabbath?

MENDEL: No—that's the curious part of it. She said that even as a boy you played your fiddle on *Shabbos*, and that if the Lord has stood it all these years, He must consider you an exception.

DAVID: You see! She's more sensible than you thought. I daresay whatever I were to do she'd consider me an exception.

MENDEL (*In sullen acquiescence*): I suppose geniuses *are*.

KATHLEEN (*Reaching them; panting with admiration and breathlessness*): Oh, Mr. David! it was like midnight mass! But the misthress was ashleep.

DAVID: Asleep!

(*Laughs half-merrily, half-sadly*)

Ha! Ha! Ha!

FRAU QUIXANO (*Panting and laughing in response*): He! He! He! *Dovidel lacht widder.* He! He! He!

(*She touches his arm affectionately, but feeling his wet coat, utters a cry of horror*)

*Du bist nass!*

DAVID: *Es ist gor nicht*, Granny—my clothes are thick.

(*She fusses over him, wiping him down with her gloved hand*)

MENDEL: But what brought you up here, Kathleen?

KATHLEEN: Sure, not the elevator. The misthress said 'twould be breaking the *Shabbos* to ride up in it.

DAVID (*Uneasily*): But did—did Miss Revendal send you up?

KATHLEEN: And who else should be axin' the misthress if she wasn't proud of Mr. David? Faith, she's a sweet lady.

MENDEL (*Impatiently*): Don't chatter, Kathleen.

KATHLEEN: But, Mr. Quixano—!

DAVID (*Sweetly*): Please take your mistress down again—don't let her walk.

KATHLEEN: But *Shabbos* isn't out yet!

MENDEL: Chattering again!

DAVID (*Gently*): There's no harm, Kathleen, in going *down* in the elevator.

KATHLEEN: Troth, I'll egshplain to her that droppin' down isn't ridin'.

DAVID (*Smiling*): Yes, tell her dropping down is natural—not *work*, like flying up.

(KATHLEEN *begins to move toward the stairs, explaining to* FRAU QUIXANO)
And, Kathleen! You'll get her some refreshments.

KATHLEEN (*Turns, glaring*): Refreshments, is it? Give her refreshments where they mix the mate with the butther plates! Oh, Mr. David!

(*She moves off toward the stairs in reproachful sorrow*)

MENDEL (*Smiling*): I'll get her some coffee.

DAVID (*Smiling*): Yes, that'll keep her awake. Besides, Pappelmeister was so sure the people wouldn't understand me, he's relaxing them on Gounod and Rossini.

MENDEL: Pappelmeister's idea of relaxation! *I* should have given them comic opera.

(*With sudden call to* KATHLEEN, *who with her mistress is at the wrong exit*)
Kathleen! The elevator's *this* side!

KATHLEEN (*Turning*): What way can that be, when I came up *this* side?

MENDEL: You chatter too much.

(FRAU QUIXANO, *not understanding, exit*)
Come this way. Can't you see the elevator?

KATHLEEN (*Perceives* FRAU QUIXANO *has gone, calls after her in Irish-sounding Yiddish*): *Wu geht Ihr*, bedad? . . .

(*Impatiently*)
Houly Moses, *komm' zurick!*

(*Exit anxiously, re-enter with* FRAU QUIXANO)
Begorra, we Jews never know our way.

(MENDEL, *carrying the violin, escorts his mother and* KATHLEEN *to the elevator. When they are near it, it stops with a thud, and* PAPPELMEISTER *springs out, his umbrella up, meeting them face to face. He looks happy and beaming over* DAVID's *triumph*)

PAPPELMEISTER (*In loud, joyous voice*): *Nun, Frau Quixano, was sagen Sie?* Vat you tink of your David?

FRAU QUIXANO: *Dovid? Er ist meshuggah.*

(*She taps her forehead*)

PAPPELMEISTER (*Puzzled, to* MENDEL): *Meshuggah!* Vat means *meshuggah?* Crazy?

MENDEL (*Half-smiling*): You've struck it. She says David doesn't know enough to go in out of the rain.

(*General laughter*)

DAVID (*Rising*): But it's stopped raining, Herr Pappelmeister. You don't want your umbrella.

(*General laughter*)

PAPPELMEISTER: *So.*

(*Shuts it down*)

MENDEL: *Herein, Mutter.*

(*He pushes* FRAU QUIXANO's *somewhat shrinking form into the elevator.* KATHLEEN *follows, then* MENDEL)

Herr Pappelmeister, we are all your grateful servants.

(PAPPELMEISTER *bows; the gates close, the elevator descends*)

DAVID: And you won't think *me* ungrateful for running away—you know my thanks are too deep to be spoken.

PAPPELMEISTER: And zo are my congratulations!

DAVID: Then, don't speak them, please.

PAPPELMEISTER: But you *must* come and speak to all de people in America who undershtand music.

DAVID (*Half-smiling*): To your four connoisseurs?

(*Seriously*)

Oh, please! I really could not meet strangers, especially musical vampires.

PAPPELMEISTER (*Half-startled, half-angry*): Vampires? Oh, come!

DAVID: Voluptuaries, then—rich, idle æsthetes to whom art and life have no connection, parasites who suck our music—

PAPPELMEISTER (*Laughs good-naturedly*): Ha! Ha! Ha! Vait till you hear vat dey say.

DAVID: I will wait as long as you like.

PAPPELMEISTER: Den I like to tell you now.

(*He roars with mischievous laughter*)

Ha! Ha! Ha! De first vampire says it is a great vork, but poorly performed.

DAVID (*Indignant*): Oh!

PAPPELMEISTER: De second vampire says it is a poor vork, but greatly performed.

DAVID (*Disappointed*): Oh!

PAPPELMEISTER: De dird vampire says it is a great vork greatly performed.

DAVID (*Complacently*): Ah!

PAPPELMEISTER: And de fourz vampire says it is a poor vork poorly performed.

DAVID (*Angry and disappointed*): Oh!

(*Then smiling*)

You see you *have* to go by the people after all.

PAPPELMEISTER (*Shakes head, smiling*): *Nein.* Ven critics disagree—I agree mit mineself. Ha! Ha! Ha!

(*He slaps* DAVID *on the back*)

A great vork dat vill be even better performed next time! Ha! Ha! Ha! Ten dousand congratulations.

(*He seizes* DAVID'S *hand and grips it heartily*)

DAVID: Don't! You hurt me.

PAPPELMEISTER (*Dropping* DAVID'S *hand,—misunderstanding*): Pardon! I forgot your vound.

DAVID: No—no—what does my wound matter? That never stung half so much as these clappings and congratulations.

PAPPELMEISTER (*Puzzled but solicitous*): I knew your nerves vould be all shnapping like fiddle-shtrings. Oh, you cheniuses!

(*Smiling*)

You like neider de clappings nor de criticisms,—*was?*

DAVID: They are equally—irrelevant. One has to wrestle with one's own art, one's own soul, *alone!*

PAPPELMEISTER (*Patting him soothingly*): I am glad I did not let you blay in Part Two.

DAVID: Dear Herr Pappelmeister! Don't think I don't appreciate all your kindnesses—you are almost a father to me.

PAPPELMEISTER: And you disobey me like a son. Ha! Ha! Ha! Vell, I vill make your excuses to de—vampires. Ha! Ha! *Also*, David.

(*He lays his hand again affectionately on* DAVID'S *right shoulder*)

*Lebe wohl!* I must go down to my popular classics.

(*Gloomily*)

Truly a going down! *Was?*

DAVID (*Smiling*): Oh, it isn't such a descent as all that. Uncle said you ought to have given them comic opera.

PAPPELMEISTER (*Shuddering convulsively*): Comic opera. . . Ouf!

(*He goes toward the elevator and rings the bell. Then he turns to* DAVID)

Vat vas dat vord, David?

DAVID: What word?

PAPPELMEISTER (*Groping for it*): Mega—megasshu. . .

DAVID (*Puzzled*): Megasshu?

(*The elevator comes up; the gates open*)

PAPPELMEISTER: *Megusshah!* You know.

(*He taps his forehead with his umbrella*)

DAVID: Ah, *meshuggah!*

PAPPELMEISTER (*Joyously*): *Ja, meshuggah!*

(*He gives a great roar of laughter*)

Ha! Ha! Ha!

(*He waves umbrella at* DAVID)

Well, don't be. . . *meshuggah.*

(*He steps into the elevator*)

Ha! Ha! Ha!

(*The gates close, and it descends with his laughter*)

DAVID (*After a pause*): Perhaps I *am*. . . *meshuggah.*

(*He walks up and down moodily, approaches the parapet at back*)

Dropping down is indeed natural.

(*He looks over*)

How it tugs and drags at one!

(*He moves back resolutely and shakes his head*)

That would be even a greater descent than Pappelmeister's to comic opera. One *must* fly upward—somehow.

(*He drops on the chair that* MENDEL *dried. A faint music steals up and makes an accompaniment to all the rest of the scene*)

Ah! the popular classics!

(*His head sinks on a little table. The elevator comes up again, but he does not raise his head.* VERA, *pale and sad, steps out and walks gently over to him; stands looking at him with maternal pity; then decides not to disturb him and is stealing away when suddenly he looks up and perceives her and springs to his feet with a dazed glad cry*)

Vera!

VERA (*Turns, speaks with grave dignity*): Miss Andrews has charged me to convey to you the heart-felt thanks and congratulations of the Settlement.

DAVID (*Frozen*): Miss Andrews is very kind. . . I trust you are well.

VERA: Thank you, Mr. Quixano. Very well and very busy. So you'll excuse me.

(*She turns to go*)

DAVID: Certainly. . . How are your folks?

VERA (*Turns her head*): They are gone back to Russia. And yours?

DAVID: You just saw them all.

VERA (*Confused*): Yes—yes—of course—I forgot! Good-bye, Mr. Quixano.

DAVID: Good-bye, Miss Revendal.

(*He drops back on the chair.* VERA *walks to the elevator, then just before ringing turns again*)

VERA: I shouldn't advise you to sit here in the damp.

DAVID: My uncle dried the chair.

(*Bitterly*)

Curious how every one is concerned about my body and no one about my soul.

VERA: Because your soul is so much stronger than your body. Why, think! It has just lifted a thousand people far higher than this roof-garden.

DAVID: Please don't you congratulate me, too! That would be too ironical.

VERA (*Agitated, coming nearer*): Irony, Mr. Quixano? Please, please, do not imagine there is any irony in my congratulations.

DAVID: The irony is in all the congratulations. How can I endure them when I know what a terrible failure I have made!

VERA: Failure! Because the critics are all divided? That is the surest proof of success. You have produced something real and new.

DAVID: I am not thinking of Pappelmeister's connoisseurs—*I* am the only connoisseur, the only one who knows. And every bar of my music cried "Failure! Failure!" It shrieked from the violins, blared from the trombones, thundered from the drums. It was written on all the faces—

VERA (*Vehemently, coming still nearer*): Oh, no! no! I watched the faces—those faces of toil and sorrow, those faces from many lands. They were fired by your vision of their coming brotherhood, lulled by your dream of their land of rest. And I could see that you were right in speaking to the people. In some strange, beautiful, way the inner meaning of your music stole into all those simple souls—

DAVID (*Springing up*): And *my* soul? What of *my* soul? False to its own music, its own mission, its own dream. That is what I mean by failure, Vera. I preached of God's Crucible, this great new continent that could melt up all race-differences and vendettas, that could purge and re-create, and God tried me with his supremest test. He gave me a heritage from the Old World, hate and vengeance and blood, and said, "Cast it all into my Crucible." And I said, "Even thy Crucible cannot melt this hate, cannot drink up this blood." And so I sat crooning over the dead past, gloating over the old blood-stains—I, the apostle of America, the prophet of the God of our children. Oh—how my music mocked me! And you—so fearless, so high above fate—how you must despise me!

VERA: I? Ah no!

DAVID: You must. You do. Your words still sting. Were it seven seas between us, you said, our love must cross them. And I—I who had prated of seven seas—

VERA: Not seas of blood—I spoke selfishly, thoughtlessly. I had not realized that crimson flood. Now I see it day and night. O God!

(*She shudders and covers her eyes*)

DAVID: There lies my failure—to have brought it to your eyes, instead of blotting it from my own.

VERA: No man could have blotted it out.

DAVID: Yes—by faith in the Crucible. From the blood of battlefields spring daisies and buttercups. In the divine chemistry the very garbage turns to roses. But in the supreme moment my faith was found wanting. You came to me—and I thrust you away.

VERA: I ought not to have come to you. . . I ought not to have come to you to-day. We must not meet again.

DAVID: Ah, you cannot forgive me!

VERA: Forgive? It is I that should go down on my knees for my father's sin.

(*She is half-sinking to her knees. He stops her by a gesture and a cry*)

DAVID: No! The sins of the fathers shall not be visited on the children.

VERA: My brain follows you, but not my heart. It is heavy with the sense of unpaid debts—debts that can only cry for forgiveness.

DAVID: You owe me nothing—

VERA: But my father, my people, my country. . .
(*She breaks down. Recovers herself*)

My only consolation is, you need nothing.

DAVID (*Dazed*): I—need—nothing?

VERA: Nothing but your music. . . your dreams.

DAVID: And your love? Do I not need that?

VERA (*Shaking her head sadly*): No.

DAVID: You say that because I have forfeited it.

VERA: It is my only consolation, I tell you, that you do not need me. In our happiest moments a suspicion of this truth used to lacerate me. But now it is my one comfort in the doom that divides us. See how you stand up here above the world, alone and self-sufficient. No woman could ever have more than the second place in your life.

DAVID: But you have the *first* place, Vera!

VERA (*Shakes her head again*): No—I no longer even desire it. I have gotten over that womanly weakness.

DAVID: You torture me. What do you mean?

VERA: What can be simpler? I used to be jealous of your music, your prophetic visions. I wanted to come first—before them all! Now, dear David, I only pray that they may fill your life to the brim.

DAVID: But they cannot.

VERA: They will—have faith in yourself, in your mission—good-bye.

DAVID (*Dazed*): You love me and you leave me?

VERA: What else can I do? Shall the shadow of Kishineff hang over all your years to come? Shall I kiss you and leave blood upon your lips, cling to you and be pushed away by all those cold, dead hands?

DAVID (*Taking both her hands*): Yes, cling to me, despite them all, cling to me till all these ghosts are exorcised, cling to me till our love triumphs over death. Kiss me, kiss me now.

VERA (*Resisting, drawing back*): I dare not! It will make you remember.

DAVID: It will make me forget. Kiss me.
(*There is a pause of hesitation, filled up by the Cathedral music from "Faust" surging up softly from below*)

VERA (*Slowly*): I will kiss you as we Russians kiss at Easter—the three kisses of peace.
(*She kisses him three times on the mouth as in ritual solemnity*)

DAVID (*Very calmly*): Easter was the date of the massacre—see! I am at peace.

VERA: God grant it endure!

ISRAEL ZANGWILL

(*They stand quietly hand in hand*)

Look! How beautiful the sunset is after the storm!

(DAVID *turns. The sunset, which has begun to grow beautiful just after* VERA'S *entrance, has now reached its most magnificent moment; below there are narrow lines of saffron and pale gold, but above the whole sky is one glory of burning flame*)

DAVID (*Prophetically exalted by the spectacle*): It is the fires of God round His Crucible.

(*He drops her hand and points downward*)

There she lies, the great Melting Pot—listen! Can't you hear the roaring and the bubbling? There gapes her mouth

(*He points east*)

—the harbour where a thousand mammoth feeders come from the ends of the world to pour in their human freight. Ah, what a stirring and a seething! Celt and Latin, Slav and Teuton, Greek and Syrian,—black and yellow—

VERA (*Softly, nestling to him*): Jew and Gentile—

DAVID: Yes, East and West, and North and South, the palm and the pine, the pole and the equator, the crescent and the cross—how the great Alchemist melts and fuses them with his purging flame! Here shall they all unite to build the Republic of Man and the Kingdom of God. Ah, Vera, what is the glory of Rome and Jerusalem where all nations and races come to worship and look back, compared with the glory of America, where all races and nations come to labour and look forward!

(*He raises his hands in benediction over the shining city*)

Peace, peace, to all ye unborn millions, fated to fill this giant continent—the God of our *children* give you Peace.

(*An instant's solemn pause. The sunset is swiftly fading, and the vast panorama is suffused with a more restful twilight, to which the many-gleaming lights of the town add the tender poetry of the night. Far back, like a lonely, guiding star, twinkles over the darkening water the torch of the Statue of Liberty. From below comes up the softened sound of voices and instruments joining in "My Country, 'tis of Thee." The curtain falls slowly*)

## Appendix A

# The Melting Pot in Action

| | |
|---|---:|
| African (black) | 9,734 |
| Armenian | 9,554 |
| Bohemian and Moravian | 11,852 |
| Bulgarian, Servian, Montenegrin | 10,083 |
| Chinese | 3,487 |
| Croatian and Slavonian | 44,754 |
| Cuban | 6,121 |
| Dalmatian, Bosnian, Herzegovinian | 4,775 |
| Dutch and Flemish | 18,746 |
| East Indian | 233 |
| English | 100,062 |
| Finnish | 14,920 |
| French | 26,509 |
| German | 101,764 |
| Greek | 40,933 |
| Hebrew | 105,826 |
| Irish | 48,103 |
| Italian (north) | 54,171 |
| Italian (south) | 264,348 |
| Japanese | 11,672 |
| Korean | 74 |
| Lithuanian | 25,529 |
| Magyar | 33,561 |
| Mexican | 15,495 |
| Pacific Islander | 27 |
| Polish | 185,207 |
| Portuguese | 14,631 |
| Roumanian | 14,780 |
| Russian | 58,380 |
| Ruthenian (Russniak) | 39,405 |
| Scandinavian | 51,650 |

| | |
|---|---:|
| Scotch | 31,434 |
| Slovak | 29,094 |
| Spanish | 15,017 |
| Spanish-American | 3,409 |
| Syrian | 10,019 |
| Turkish | 2,132 |
| Welsh | 3,922 |
| West Indian (except Cuban) | 2,302 |
| Other peoples | 3,512 |
| | |
| Total | 1,427,227 |

# Appendix B

# The Pogrom

## (I) A Russian on its Reasons

(From *The Nation*, November 15, 1913)
It is now over thirty years since the crew of the sinking ship of Russian absolutism first tried this unworthy weapon to save their failing cause. This was when Plehve organised an anti-Semitic agitation and Jewish pogroms in 1883 in South Russia, where the Jews formed almost the only merchant class in the villages, and where the ignorant peasants, together with some crafty Russian tradesmen, had a natural grudge against them. The result was that the prevailing discontent of the masses was diverted against the Jews. A large public meeting of protest was organised at that time in the London Mansion House, the Lord Mayor taking the chair. English public opinion rightly appreciated the value of this criminal method of using Jews as scapegoats for political purposes. Now we see merely a further, and let us hope a final, development of the same tactics. They have been used on many occasions since 1883. One of the largest Jewish pogroms of the latest series in Kishineff in 1903 has been clearly traced to the same experienced hand of Plehve, when the passive attitude of the local administration and the military was explained by the presence in the town of a mysterious colonel of the Imperial Gendarmerie who arrived with secret orders and a large supply of pogrom literature from St. Petersburg, and who organised the scum of the town population for the purpose of looting and killing Jews.

The repulsive stories of further pogroms all over the country immediately after the issue of the constitutional manifesto of October 17, 1905, are fresh in the memory of the civilised world. At that time anti-Semitic doctrine was openly preached, not only against Jews, but against the whole constitutional and revolutionary upheaval. Pogroms against both were organised under the same pretext of saving the Tsar, the orthodoxy, and the Fatherland. Local police and military officials had secret orders to abstain from interference with the looting and murdering of Jews or "their hirelings." Processions of peaceful citizens and children were trampled down by the Cossack horses, and the Cossacks received formal thanks from high quarters for their excellent exploits. . .

N. W. Tchaykovsky

### (II) A Nurse on its Results

(From Public Health, Nurses' Quarterly,<br>Cleveland, Ohio, October 1913)

I was a Red Cross nurse on the battlefield.

The words of the chief doctor of the Jewish Hospital of Odessa still ring in my ears. When the telephone message came, he said, "Moldvanko is running in blood; send nurses and doctors." This meant that the Pogrom (massacre) was going on.

Dr. P—— came into the wards with these words: "Sisters, there is no time for weeping. Those who have no one dependent upon them, come. Put on your white surgical gowns, and the red cross. Make ready to go on the battlefield at once. God knows how many of our sisters and brothers are already killed." Tears were just running down his cheeks as he spoke. In a minute twelve nurses and eight doctors had volunteered. There was one Red Cross nurse who was in bed waiting to be operated on. She got up and made ready too. Nobody could keep her from going with us. "Where my sisters and brothers fall, there shall I fall," she said, and with these words, jumped into the ambulance and went on to the City Hospital with us. There they had better equipment, and they sent out three times as many nurses as the Jewish Hospital. At the City Hospital they hung silver crosses about our necks. We wore the silver crosses so that we would not be recognised as Jewish by the Holiganes (Hooligans).

Then we went to Molorosiskia Street in the Moldvanko (slums). We could not see, for the feathers were flying like snow. The blood was already up to our ankles on the pavement and in the yards. The uproar was deafening but we could hear the Holiganes' fierce cries of "Hooray, kill the Jews," on all sides. It was enough to hear such words. They could turn your hair grey, but we went on. We had no time to think. All our thoughts were to pick up wounded ones, and to try to rescue some uninjured ones. We succeeded in rescuing some uninjured who were in hiding. We put bandages on them to make it appear that they were wounded. We put them in the ambulance and carried them to the hospital, too. So at the Jewish Hospital we had five thousand injured and seven thousand uninjured to feed and protect for two weeks.

Some were left without homes, without clothes, and children were even without parents.

My dear reader, I want to tell you one thing before I describe the scenes of the massacre any further; do not think that you are reading a story which could not happen! No, I want you to know that everything you read is just exactly as it was. My hair is a little grey, but I am surprised it is not quite white after what I witnessed.

The procession of the Pogrom was led by about ten Catholic (Greek) Sisters with about forty or fifty of their school children. They carried ikons or pictures of Jesus and sang "God Save the Tsar." They were followed by a crowd containing hundreds of men and women murderers yelling "Bey Zhida," which means "Kill the Jews." With these words they ran into the yards where there were fifty or a hundred tenants. They rushed in like tigers. Soon they began to throw children out of the windows of the second, third, and fourth stories. They would take a poor, innocent six-months-old baby, who could not possibly have done any harm in this world and throw it down on to the pavement. You can imagine it could not live after it struck the ground, but this did not satisfy the stony-hearted murderers. They then rushed up to the child, seized it and broke its little arm and leg bones into three or four pieces, then wrung its neck too. They laughed and yelled, so carried away with pleasure at their successful work.

I do wish a few Americans could have been there to see, and they would know what America is, and what it means to live in the United States. It was not enough for them to open up a woman's abdomen and take out the child which she carried, but they took time to stuff the abdomen with straw and fill it up. Can you imagine human beings able to do such things? I do not think anybody could, because I could not imagine it myself when a few years before I read the news of the massacre in Kishineff, but now I have seen it with my own eyes. It was not enough for them to cut out an old man's tongue and cut off his nose, but they drove nails into the eyes also. You wonder how they had enough time to carry away everything of value—money, gold, silver, jewels—and still be able to do so much fancy killing, but oh, my friends, all the time for three days and three nights was theirs.

The last day and night it poured down rain, and you would think that might stop them, but no, they worked just as hard as ever. We could wear shoes no longer. Our feet were swollen, so we wore rubbers over our stockings, and in this way worked until some power was able to stop these horrors. They not only killed, but they had time to abuse young girls of twelve and fourteen years of age, who died immediately after being operated upon.

I remember what happened to my own class-mates. They were two who came from a small town to Odessa to become midwives. These girls ran to the school to hide themselves as it was a government school, and they knew the Holiganes would not dare to come in there. But the dean of the school had ordered they should not be admitted, because they were Jewish, as if they had different blood running in their veins. So when they came, the watchman refused to open the doors, according to his instructions. The crowd of Holiganes found them outside the doors of the hospital. They abused them right there in the middle of the street. One was eighteen years old and the other was twenty. One died after the operation and the other went insane from shame.

Some people ask why the Jews did not leave everything and go away. But how could they go and where could they go? The murderers were scattered throughout the Jewish quarters. All they could do was hide where they were in the cellars and garrets. The Holiganes searched them out and killed them where they were hidden. Others may ask, why did they not resist the murderers with their knives and pistols? The grown men organised by the second day. They were helped by the Vigilantes, too, who brought them arms. The Vigilantes were composed of students at the University and high-school boys, and also the strongest man from each Jewish family. There were a good many Gentiles among the students who belonged to the Vigilantes because they wanted justice. So on the second day the Vigilantes stood before the doors and gave resistance to the murderers. Some will ask where were the soldiers and the police? They were sent to protect, but on arriving, joined in with the murderers. However, the police put disguises on over their uniforms. Later, when they were brought to the hospital with other wounded, we found their uniforms underneath their disguises.

When the Vigilantes took their stations, the scene was like a battlefield. Bullets were flying from both sides of the Red Cross carriages. We expected to be killed any minute, but notwithstanding, we rushed wherever there were shots heard in order to carry away the wounded. Whenever we arrived we shouted "Red Cross, Red Cross," in order to help make them realise we were not Vigilantes. Then they would stop and let us pick up the wounded. They did this on account of their own wounded.

The Vigilantes could not stop the butchery entirely because they were not strong enough in numbers. On the fourth day, the Jewish people of Odessa, through Dr. P——, succeeded in communicating to the Mayor of a different State. Soldiers from outside, strangers to the murderers, came in and took charge of the city. The city was put under martial law until order could be restored.

On the fifth day the doctors and nurses were called to the cemetery, where there were four hundred unidentified dead. Their friends and relatives who came to search for them were crazed and hysterical and needed our attention. Wives came to look for husbands, parents hunting children, a mother for her only son, and so on. It took eight days to identify the bodies and by that time four hundred of the wounded had died, and so we had eight hundred to bury. If you visit Odessa, you will be shown two long graves, about one hundred feet long, beside the Jewish Cemetery. There lie the victims of the massacre. Among them are Gentile Vigilantes whose parents asked that they be buried with the Jews. . .

Another case I knew was that of a married man. He left his wife, who was pregnant, and three children, to go on a business trip. When he got back the massacre had occurred. His home was in ruins, his family gone. He went to the hospital, then to the cemetery. There he found his wife with her abdomen stuffed with straw, and his three children dead. It simply broke his heart, and he lost his mind. But he was harmless, and was to be seen wandering about the hospital as though in search of some one, and daily he grew more thin and suffering.

This story is told in the hope that Americans will appreciate the safety and freedom in which they live and that they will help others to gain that freedom.

# Appendix C

## THE STORY OF DANIEL MELSA

Another example of Nature aping Art is afforded by the romantic story of Daniel Melsa, a young Russo-Jewish violinist who has carried audiences by storm in Berlin, Paris and London, and who had arranged to go to America last November. The following extract from an interview in the *Jewish Chronicle* of January 24, 1913, shows the curious coincidence between his beginnings and David Quixano's:

"Melsa is not yet twenty years of age, but he looks somewhat older. He is of slight build and has a sad expression, which increased to almost a painful degree when recounting some of his past experiences. He seems singularly devoid of any affectation, while modesty is obviously the keynote of his nature.

"After some persuasion, Melsa put aside his reticence, and, complying with the request, outlined briefly his career, the early part of which, he said, was overshadowed by a great tragedy. He was born in Warsaw, and, at the age of three, his parents moved to Lodz, where shortly after a private tutor was engaged for him.

"'Although I exhibited a passion for music quite early, I did not receive any lessons on the subject till my seventh birthday, but before that my father obtained a cheap violin for me upon which I was soon able to play simple melodies by ear.'

"By chance a well-known professor of the town heard him play, and so impressed was he with the talent exhibited by the boy that he advised the father to have him educated. Acting upon this advice, as far as limited means allowed, tutors were engaged, and so much progress did he make that at the age of nine he was admitted to the local Conservatorium of Professor Grudzinski, where he remained two years. It was at the age of eleven that a great calamity overtook the family, his father and sister falling victims to the pogroms.

"Melsa's story runs as follows:

"'It was in June of 1905, at the time of the pogroms, when one afternoon my father, accompanied by my little sister, ventured out into the street, from which they never returned. They were both killed,' he added sadly, 'by Cossacks. A week later I found my sister in a Christian churchyard riddled with bullets, but I have not been able to trace the remains of my father, who must have been buried in some out-of-the-way place. During this awful period my mother and myself lived in imminent danger of our lives, and it was only the recollection of my playing that saved us also falling a prey to the vodka-besodden Cossacks.'"

# Appendix D

## BEILIS AND AMERICA

The close relation in Jewish thought between Russo-Jewish persecution and America as the land of escape from it is well illustrated by the recent remarks of the *Jewish Chronicle* on the future of the victim of the Blood-Ritual Prosecution in Kieff. "So long as Beilis continues to live in Russia, his life is unsafe. The Black Hundreds, he himself says, have solemnly decided on his death, and we have seen, in the not distant past, that they can carry out diabolical plots of this description with complete immunity. . . He would gladly go to America, provided he was sure of a living. The condition should not be difficult to fulfil, and if this victim of a barbarous *régime*—we cannot say latest victim, for, as we write, comes the news of an expulsion order against 1200 Jewish students of Kieff—should find a home and place under the sheltering wing of freedom, it would be a fitting ending to a painful chapter in our Jewish history."

That it is the natural ending even the Jew-baiting Russian organ, the *Novoe Vremya*, indirectly testifies, for it has published a sneering cartoon representing a number of Jews crowded on the Statue of Liberty to welcome the arrival of Beilis. One wonders that the Russian censor should have permitted the masses to become aware that Liberty exists on earth, if only in the form of a statue.

# Appendix E

## The Alien in the Melting Pot

Mr. Frederick J. Haskin has recently published in the *Chicago Daily News* the following graphic summary of what immigrants have done and do for the United States:

I am the immigrant.

Since the dawn of creation my restless feet have beaten new paths across the earth.

My uneasy bark has tossed on all seas.

My wanderlust was born of the craving for more liberty and a better wage for the sweat of my face.

I looked towards the United States with eyes kindled by the fire of ambition and heart quickened with new-born hope.

I approached its gates with great expectation.

I entered in with fine hopes.

I have shouldered my burden as the American man of all work.

I contribute eighty-five per cent. of all the labour in the slaughtering and meat-packing industries.

I do seven-tenths of the bituminous coal mining.

I do seventy-eight per cent. of all the work in the woollen mills.

I contribute nine-tenths of all the labour in the cotton mills.

I make nine-twentieths of all the clothing.

I manufacture more than half the shoes.

I build four-fifths of all the furniture.

I make half of the collars, cuffs, and shirts.

I turn out four-fifths of all the leather.

I make half the gloves.

I refine nearly nineteen-twentieths of the sugar.

I make half of the tobacco and cigars.

And yet, I am the great American problem.

When I pour out my blood on your altar of labour, and lay down my life as a sacrifice to your god of toil, men make no more comment than at the fall of a sparrow.

But my brawn is woven into the warp and woof of the fabric of your national being.

My children shall be your children and your land shall be my land because my sweat and my blood will cement the foundations of the America of To-Morrow.

If I can be fused into the body politic, the Melting-Pot will have stood the supreme test.

# AFTERWORD

## I

*THE MELTING POT* IS THE third of the writer's plays to be published in book form, though the first of the three in order of composition. But unlike *The War God* and *The Next Religion*, which are dramatisations of the spiritual duels of our time, *The Melting Pot* sprang directly from the author's concrete experience as President of the Emigration Regulation Department of the Jewish Territorial Organisation, which, founded shortly after the great massacres of Jews in Russia, will soon have fostered the settlement of ten thousand Russian Jews in the West of the United States.

"Romantic claptrap," wrote Mr. A. B. Walkley in the *Times* of "this rhapsodising over music and crucibles and statues of Liberty." As if these things were not the homeliest of realities, and rhapsodising the natural response to them of the Russo-Jewish psychology, incurably optimist. The statue of Liberty is a large visible object at the mouth of New York harbour; the crucible, if visible only to the eye of imagination like the inner reality of the sunrise to the eye of Blake, is none the less a roaring and flaming actuality. These things are as substantial, if not as important, as Adeline Genée and Anna Pavlova, the objects of Mr. Walkley's own rhapsodising. Mr. Walkley, never having lacked Liberty, nor cowered for days in a cellar in terror of a howling mob, can see only theatrical exaggeration in the enthusiasm for a land of freedom, just as, never having known or never having had eyes to see the grotesque and tragic creatures existing all around us, he has doubted the reality of some of Balzac's creations. It is to be feared that for such a play as *The Melting Pot* Mr. Walkley is far from being the χαρίεις of Aristotle. The ideal spectator must have known and felt more of life than Mr. Walkley, who resembles too much the library-fed man of letters whose denunciation by Walter Bagehot he himself quotes without suspecting *de te fabula narratur*. Even the critic, who has to deal with a refracted world, cannot dispense with primary experience of his own. For "the adventures of a soul among masterpieces" it is not only necessary there should be masterpieces, there must also be a soul. Mr. Walkley, one of the wittiest of contemporary writers and within his urban range one of the wisest, can scarcely be accused of lacking a soul, though Mr. Bernard Shaw's long-enduring misconception of him as a brother in the spirit is one of the comedies of literature. But such spiritual vitality as Oxford failed to sterilise in him has been largely torpified by his profession of play-taster, with its divorcement from reality in the raw. His cry of "romantic claptrap" is merely the reaction of the club armchair to the "drums and tramplings" of the street. It is in fact (he will welcome an allusion to Dickens almost as much as one to Aristotle) the higher Podsnappery. "Thus happily acquainted with his own merit and importance, Mr. Podsnap settled that whatever he put behind him he put out of existence. . . The world got up at eight, shaved close at a quarter past, breakfasted at nine, went to the City at ten, came home at half-past five, and dined at seven."

Mr. Roosevelt, with his multifarious American experience as soldier and cowboy, hunter and historian, police-captain and President, comes far nearer the ideal spectator, for this play at least, than Mr. Walkley. Yet his enthusiasm for it has been dismissed by our critic as "stupendous *naïveté*." Mr. Roosevelt apparently falls under that class of "people who knowing no rules, are at the mercy of their undisciplined taste," which Mr. Walkley excludes altogether from his classification of critics, in despite of Dr. Johnson's opinion that "natural judges" are only second to "those who know but are above the rules." It is comforting, therefore, to find Mr. Augustus Thomas, the famous American playwright, who is familiar with the rules to the point of contempt, chivalrously associating himself, in defence of a British rival, with Mr. Roosevelt's "stupendous *naïveté*."

"Mr. Zangwill's 'rhapsodising' over music and crucibles and statues of Liberty is," says Mr. Thomas, "a very effective use of a most potent symbolism, and I have never seen men and women more sincerely stirred than the audience at *The Melting Pot*. The impulses awakened by the Zangwill play were those of wide human sympathy, charity, and compassion; and, for my own part, I would rather retire from the theatre and retire from all direct or indirect association with journalism than write down the employment of these factors by Mr. Zangwill as mere claptrap."

"As a work of art for art's sake," also wrote Mr. William Archer, "the play simply does not exist." He added: "but Mr. Zangwill would not dream of appealing to such a standard." Mr. Archer had the misfortune to see the play in New York side by side with his more cynical *confrère*, and thus his very praise has an air of apologia to Mr. Walkley and the great doctrine of "art for art's sake." It would almost seem as if he even takes a "work of art" and a "work of art for art's sake" as synonymous. Nothing, in fact, could be more inartistic. "Art for art's sake" is one species of art, whose right to existence the author has amply recognised in other works. (*The King of Schnorrers* was even read aloud by Oscar Wilde to a duchess.) But he roundly denies that art is any the less artistic for being inspired by life, and seeking in its turn to inspire life. Such a contention is tainted by the very Philistinism it would repudiate, since it seeks a negative test of art in something outside art—to wit, purpose, whose presence is surely as irrelevant to art as its absence. The only test of art is artistic quality, and this quality *occurs* perhaps more frequently than it is achieved, as in the words of the Hebrew prophets, or the vision of a slum at night, the former consciously aiming at something quite different, the latter achieving its beauty in utter unconsciousness.

## II

IT WILL BE SEEN FROM the official table of immigration that the Russian Jew is only one and not even the largest of the fifty elements that, to the tune of nearly a million and a half a year, are being fused in the greatest "Melting Pot" the world has ever known; but if he has been selected as the typical immigrant, it is because he alone of all the fifty has no homeland. Some few other races, such as the Armenians, are almost equally devoid of political power, and, in consequence, equally obnoxious to massacre; but except the gipsy, whose essence is to be homeless, there is no other race—black, white, red, or yellow—that has not remained at least a majority of the population in some area of its own. There is none, therefore, more in need of a land of liberty, none to whose future it is more vital that America should preserve that spirit of William Penn which President Wilson has so nobly characterised. And there is assuredly none which has more valuable elements to contribute to the ethnic and psychical amalgam of the people of to-morrow.

The process of American amalgamation is not assimilation or simple surrender to the dominant type, as is popularly supposed, but an all-round give-and-take by which the final type may be enriched or impoverished. Thus the intelligent reader will have remarked how the somewhat anti-Semitic Irish servant of the first act talks Yiddish herself in the fourth. Even as to the ultimate language of the United States, it is unreasonable to suppose that American, though fortunately protected by English literature, will not bear traces of the fifty languages now being spoken side by side with it, and of which this play alone presents scraps in German, French, Russian, Yiddish, Irish, Hebrew, and Italian.

That in the crucible of love, or even co-citizenship, the most violent antitheses of the past may be fused into a higher unity is a truth of both ethics and observation, and it was in order to present historic enmities at their extremes that the persecuted Jew of Russia and the persecuting Russian race have been taken for protagonists—"the fell incensèd points of mighty opposites."

The Jewish immigrant is, moreover, the toughest of all the white elements that have been poured into the American crucible, the race having, by its unique experience of several thousand years of exposure to alien majorities, developed a salamandrine power of survival. And this asbestoid fibre is made even more fireproof by the anti-Semitism of American uncivilisation. Nevertheless, to suppose that America will remain permanently afflicted by all the old European diseases would be to despair of humanity, not to mention super-humanity.

## III

EVEN THE NEGROPHOBIA IS NOT likely to remain eternally at its present barbarous pitch. Mr. William Archer, who has won a new fame as student of that black problem, which is America's nemesis for her ancient slave-raiding, and who favours the creation of a Black State as one of the United States, observes: "It is noteworthy that neither David Quixano nor anyone else in the play makes the slightest reference to that inconvenient element in the crucible of God—the negro." This is an oversight of Mr. Archer's, for Baron Revendal defends the Jew-baiting of Russia by asking of an American: "Don't you lynch and roast your niggers?" And David Quixano expressly throws both "black and yellow" into the crucible. No doubt there is an instinctive antipathy which tends to keep the white man free from black blood, though this antipathy having been overcome by a large minority in all the many periods and all the many countries of their contiguity, it is equally certain that there are at work forces of attraction as well as of repulsion, and that even upon the negro the "Melting Pot" of America will not fail to act in a measure as it has acted on the Red Indian, who has found it almost as facile to mate with his white neighbours as with his black. Indeed, it is as much social prejudice as racial antipathy that to-day divides black and white in the New World; and Sir Sydney Olivier has recorded that in Jamaica the white is far more on his guard and his dignity against the half-white than against the all-black, while in Guiana, according to Sir Harry Johnston in his great work "The Negro in the New World," it is the half-white that, in his turn, despises the black and succeeds in marrying still further whitewards. It might have been thought that the dark-white races on the northern shore of the Mediterranean—the Spaniards, Sicilians, &c.—who have already been crossed with the sons of Ham from its southern shore, would, among the American immigrants, be the natural links towards the fusion of white and black, but a similar instinct of pride and peril seems to hold them back. But whether the antipathy in America be a race instinct or a social prejudice, the accusations against the black are largely panic-born myths, for the alleged repulsive smell of the negro is consistent with being shaved by him, and the immorality of the negress is consistent with her control of the nurseries of the South. The devil is not so black nor the black so devilish as he is painted. This is not to deny that the prognathous face is an ugly and undesirable type of countenance or that it connotes a lower average of intellect and ethics, or that white and black are as yet too far apart for profitable fusion. Melanophobia, or fear of the black, may be pragmatically as valuable a racial defence for the white as the counter-instinct of philoleucosis, or love of the white, is a force of racial uplifting for the black. But neither colour has succeeded in monopolising all the virtues and graces in its specific evolution from the common ancestral ape, and a superficial acquaintance with the work of Dr. Arthur Keith teaches that if the black man is nearer the ape in some ways (having even the remains of throat-pouches), the white man is nearer in other ways (as in his greater hairiness).

And besides being, as Sir Sydney Olivier says, "a matrix of emotional and spiritual energies that have yet to find their human expression," the African negro has obviously already not a few valuable ethnic elements—joy of life, love of colour, keen senses, beautiful voice, and ear for music—contributions that might somewhat compensate for the dragging-down of the white and, in small doses at least, might one day prove a tonic to an anæmic and art-less America. A musician like Coleridge-Taylor is no despicable product of the "Melting Pot," while the negroes of genius whom the writer has been privileged to know—men like Henry O. Tanner, the painter, and Paul Laurence Dunbar, the poet—show the potentialities of the race even without white admixture; and as men of this stamp are capable of attracting cultured white wives, the fusing process, beginning at the top with types like these, should be far less unwelcome than that which starts with the dregs of both races. But the negroid hair and complexion being, in Mendelian language, "dominant," these black traits are not easy to eliminate from the hybrid posterity; and in view of all the unpleasantness, both immediate and contingent, that attends the blending of colours, only heroic souls on either side should dare the adventure of intermarriage. Blacks of this temper, however, would serve their race better by making Liberia a success or building up an American negro State, as Mr. William Archer recommends, or at least asserting their rights as American citizens in that sub-tropical South which without their labour could never have been opened up. Meantime, however scrupulously and justifiably America avoids physical intermarriage with the negro, the comic spirit cannot fail to note the spiritual miscegenation which, while clothing, commercialising, and Christianising the ex-African, has given "rag-time" and the sex-dances that go to it, first to white America and thence to the whole white world.

The action of the crucible is thus not exclusively physical—a consideration particularly important as regards the Jew. The Jew may be Americanised and the American Judaised without any gamic interaction.

## IV

AMONG THE JEWS *THE MELTING Pot*, though it has in some instances served to interpret to each other the old generation and the new, has more frequently been misunderstood by both. While a distinguished Christian clergyman wrote that it was "calculated to do for the Jewish race what 'Uncle Tom's Cabin' did for the coloured man," the Jewish pulpits of America have resounded with denunciation of its supposed solution of the Jewish problem by dissolution. As if even a play with a purpose could do more than suggest and interpret! It is true that its leading figure, David Quixano, advocates absorption in America, but even he is speaking solely of the American Jews and asks his uncle why, if he objects to the dissolving process, he did not work for a separate Jewish land. He is not offering a panacea for the Jewish problem, universally applicable. But he urges that the conditions offered to the Jew in America are without parallel throughout the world.

And, in sooth, the Jew is here citizen of a republic without a State religion—a republic resting, moreover, on the same simple principles of justice and equal rights as the Mosaic Commonwealth from which the Puritan Fathers drew their inspiration. In America, therefore, the Jew, by a roundabout journey from Zion, has come into his own again. It is by no mere accident that when an inscription was needed for the colossal statue of Liberty in New York Harbour, that "Mother of Exiles" whose torch lights the entrance to the New Jerusalem, the best expression of the spirit of Americanism was found in the sonnet of the Jewess, Emma Lazarus:

> *Give me your tired, your poor,*
> *Your huddled masses yearning to breathe free,*
> *The wretched refuse of your teeming shore.*
> *Send these, the homeless, tempest-tost to me,*
> *I lift my lamp beside the golden door.*

And if, alas! passing through the golden door, the Jew finds his New Jerusalem as much a caricature by the crumbling of its early ideals as the old became by the fading of the visions of Isaiah and Amos, he may find his mission in fighting for the preservation of the original Hebraic pattern. In this fight he will not be alone, and intermarriage with his fellow-crusaders in the new Land of Promise will naturally follow wherever, as with David Quixano and Vera Revendal, no theological differences divide. There will be neither Jew nor Greek. Intermarriage, wherever there is social intimacy, will follow, even when the parties stand in opposite religious camps; but this is less advisable as leading to a house divided against itself and to dissension in the upbringing of the children. It is only when a common outlook has been reached, transcending the old doctrinal differences, that intermarriage is denuded of those latent discords which the instinct of mankind divines, and which keep even Catholic and Protestant wisely apart.

These discords, together with the prevalent anti-Semitism and his own ingrained persistence, tend to preserve the Jew even in the "Melting Pot," so that his dissolution must be necessarily slower than that of the similar aggregations of Germans, Italians, or Poles. But the process for all is the same, however tempered by specific factors. Beginning as broken-off bits of Germany, Italy, or Poland, with newspapers and theatres in German, Italian, or Polish, these colonies gradually become Americanised, their vernaculars, even when jealously cherished, become a mere medium for American conceptions of life; while in the third generation the child is ashamed both of its parents and their lingo, the newspapers dwindle in circulation, the theatres languish. The reality of this process has been denied by no less distinguished an American than Dr. Charles Eliot, ex-President of Harvard University, whose prophecy of Jewish solidarity in America and of the contribution of Judaism to the world's future is more optimistic than my own. Dr. Eliot points to the still unmelted heaps of racial matter, without suspecting—although he is a chemist—that their semblance of solidity is only kept up by the constant immigration of similar atoms to the base to replace those liquefied at the apex. Once America slams her doors, the crucible will roar like a closed furnace.

Heaven forbid, however, that the doors shall be slammed for centuries yet. The notion that the few millions of people in America have a moral right to exclude others is monstrous. Exclusiveness may have some justification in countries, especially when old and well-populated; but for continents like the United States—or for the matter of that Canada and Australia—to mistake themselves for mere countries is an intolerable injustice to the rest of the human race.

The exclusion of criminals even is as impossible in practice as the exclusion of the sick and ailing is unchristian. Infinitely more important were it to keep the gates of *birth* free from undesirables. As for the exclusion of the able-bodied, whether illiterate or literate, that is sheer economic madness in so empty a continent, especially with the Panama Canal to divert them to the least developed States. Fortunately, any serious restriction will avenge itself not only by the stagnation of many of the States, but by the paralysis of the great liners which depend on steerage passengers, without whom freights and fares will rise and saloon passengers be docked of their sailing facilities. Meantime the inquisition at Ellis Island has to its account cruelties no less atrocious than the ancient Spanish—cruelties that only flash into momentary prominence when some luxurious music-hall lady of dubious morals has a taste of the barbarities meted out daily to blameless and hard-working refugees from oppression or hunger, who, having staked their all on the great adventure, find themselves hustled back, penniless and heartbroken, to the Old World.

## V

WHETHER ANY COUNTRY WILL EVER again be based like those of the Old World upon a unity of race or religion is a matter of doubt.

New England, of course, like Pennsylvania and Maryland, owes its inception to religion, but the original impulse has long been submerged by purely economic pressures. And the same motley immigration from the Old World is building up the bulk of the coming countries. At most, the dominant language gives a semblance of unity and serves to attract a considerable stream of immigrants who speak it, as of Portuguese to Brazil, Spaniards to the Argentine. But the chief magnet remains economic, for Brazil draws six times as many Italians as Portuguese, and the Argentine two and a half times as many Italians as Spanish. It may be urged, of course, that the Italian gravitation to these countries is still a matter of race, and that, in the absence of an El Dorado of his own, the Italian is attracted towards States that are at least Latin. But though Brazil and the Argentine be predominantly Latin, the minority of Germans, Austrians, and Swiss is by no means insignificant. The great modern steamship, in fact—supplemented by its wandering and seductive agent—is playing the part in the world formerly played by invasions and crusades, while the "economic" immigrant is more and more replacing the refugee, just as the purely commercial company working under native law is replacing the Chartered Company which was a law to itself. How small a part in the modern movement is played by patriotism proper may be seen from the avidity with which the farmers of the United States cross the borders to Canada to obtain the large free holdings which enable them to sell off their American properties. How little the proudest tradition counts against the environment is shown in the shame felt by Argentine-born children for the English spoken by their British parents.

The difference in the method of importing the ingredients makes thus no difference to the action of the crucible. Though the peoples now in process of formation in the New World are being recruited by mainly economic forces, it may be predicted they will ultimately harden into homogeneity of race, if not even of belief. For internationalism in religion seems to be again receding in favour of national religions (if, indeed, these were ever more than superficially superseded), at any rate in favour of nationalism raised into religion.

If racial homogeneity has not yet been evolved completely even in England—and, of course, the tendency can never be more than asymptotic—it is because cheap and easy transport and communication, with freedom of economic movement, have been late developments and are still far from perfect. Hence, there has never been a thorough shake-up and admixture of elements, so that certain counties and corners have retained types and breeds peculiar to them. But with the ever-growing interconnection of all parts of the country, and with the multiplication of labour bureaux, these breeds and types will be—alas, for local colour!—increasingly absorbed in the general mass. For fusion and unification are part of the historic life-process. "Normans and Saxons and Danes" are we here in England, yes and Huguenots and Flemings and Gascons and Angevins and Jews and many other things.

In fact, according to Sir Harry Johnston, there is hardly an ethnic element that has not entered into the Englishman, including even the missing link, as the Piltdown skull would seem to testify. The earlier discovery at Galley Hill showed Britannia rising from the apes with an extinct Tasmanian type, not unlike the surviving aboriginal Australian. Then the west of Britain was invaded by a negroid type from France followed by an Eskimo type of which traces are still to be seen in the West of Ireland and parts of Scotland. Next came the true Mediterranean white man, the Iberian, with dark hair and eyes and a white skin; and then the round-headed people of the Bronze Age, probably Asiatic. And then the Gael, the long-headed, fair-haired Aryan, who ruled by iron and whose Keltic vocabulary was tinged with Iberian, and who was followed by the Brython or Belgian. And, at some unknown date, we have to allow for the invasion of North Britain by another Germanic type, the Caledonian, which would seem to have been a Norse stock, foreshadowing the later Norman Conquest. And, as if this mish-mash was not confusion enough, came to make it worse confounded the Roman conquerors, trailing like a mantle of many colours the subject-races of their far-flung Empire.

Is it wonderful if the crucible, capable of fusing such a motley of types into "the true-born Briton," should be melting up its Jews like old silver? The comparison belongs to Mr. Walkley, who was more moved by the beauty of the old and the pathos of its passing than by the resplendence of the new, and who seemed to forget that it is for the dramatist to register both impartially—their conflict constituting another of those spiritual duels which are peculiarly his affair. Jews are, unlike negroes, a "recessive" type, whose physical traits tend to disappear in the blended offspring. There does not exist in England to-day a single representative of the Jewish families whom Cromwell admitted, though their lineage may be traced in not a few noble families. Thus every country has been and is a "Melting Pot." But America, exhibiting the normal fusing process magnified many thousand diameters and diversified beyond all historic experience, and fed not by successive waves of immigration but by a hodge-podge of simultaneous hordes, is, in Bacon's phrase, an "ostensive instance" of a universal phenomenon. America is *the* "Melting Pot."

Her people has already begun to take on such a complexion of its own, it is already so emphatically tending to a new race, crossed with every European type, that the British illusion of a cousinly Anglo-Saxon people with whom war is unthinkable is sheer wilful blindness. Even to-day, while the mixture is still largely mechanical not chemical, the Anglo-Saxon element is only preponderant; it is very far from being the sum total.

VI

WHILE OUR SLUGGISH AND SENSUAL English stage has resisted and even burked the writer's attempt to express in terms of the theatre our European problems of war and religion, and to interpret through art the "years of the modern, years of the unperformed," it remains to be acknowledged with gratitude that this play, designed to bring home to America both its comparative rawness and emptiness and its true significance and potentiality for history and civilisation, has been universally acclaimed by Americans as a revelation of Americanism, despite that it contains only one native-born American character, and that a bad one. Played throughout the length and breadth of the States since its original production in 1908, given, moreover, in Universities and Women's Colleges, passing through edition after edition in book form, cited by preachers and journalists, politicians and Presidential candidates, even calling into existence a "Melting Pot" Club in Boston, it has had the happy fortune to contribute its title to current thought, and, in the testimony of Jane Addams, to "perform a great service to America by reminding us of the high hopes of the founders of the Republic."

I. Z.
*January 1914*

# A Note About the Author

Israel Zangwill (1864–1926) was a British writer. Born in London, Zangwill was raised in a family of Jewish immigrants from the Russian Empire. Alongside his brother Louis, a novelist, Zangwill was educated at the Jews' Free School in Spitalfields, where he studied secular and religious subjects. He excelled early on and was made a teacher in his teens before studying for his BA at the University of London. After graduating in 1884, Zangwill began publishing under various pseudonyms, finding editing work with *Ariel* and *The London Puck* to support himself. His first novel, *Children of the Ghetto: A Study of Peculiar People* (1892), was published to popular and critical acclaim, earning praise from prominent Victorian novelist George Gissing. His play *The Melting Pot* (1908) was a resounding success in the United States and was regarded by Theodore Roosevelt as "among the very strong and real influences upon (his) thought and (his) life." He spent his life in dedication to various political and social causes. An early Zionist and follower of Theodor Herzl, he later withdrew his support in favor of territorialism after he discovered that "Palestine proper has already its inhabitants." Despite distancing himself from the Zionist community, he continued to advocate on behalf of the Jewish people and to promote the ideals of feminism alongside his wife Edith Ayrton, a prominent author and activist.

# A Note from the Publisher

Spanning many genres, from non-fiction essays to literature classics to children's books and lyric poetry, Mint Edition books showcase the master works of our time in a modern new package. The text is freshly typeset, is clean and easy to read, and features a new note about the author in each volume. Many books also include exclusive new introductory material. Every book boasts a striking new cover, which makes it as appropriate for collecting as it is for gift giving. Mint Edition books are only printed when a reader orders them, so natural resources are not wasted. We're proud that our books are never manufactured in excess and exist only in the exact quantity they need to be read and enjoyed.

# Discover more of your favorite classics with Bookfinity™.

- Track your reading with custom book lists.
- Get great book recommendations for your personalized Reader Type.
- Add reviews for your favorite books.
- AND MUCH MORE!

Visit **bookfinity.com** and take the fun Reader Type quiz to get started.

Enjoy our classic and modern companion pairings!